"With scholarly depth and pastoral sensitivity, Carroll helps us understand not only the complex dimensions of migration but also how it brings us face-to-face with the crucified and risen Lord in our midst. Taking us beyond polarizing debates, he examines our current policies in light of biblical faith and the gifts and challenges of the reign of God. As one of the most astute and articulate scholars on the Bible and migration, Carroll calls us to contemplate the God who migrated to us in the incarnation and who calls us to move into a new way of thinking and a new relationship with all those we define as 'the other.'"

—Daniel G. Groody, CSC, University of Notre Dame

"Carroll asks, 'In a world where over 270 million people are on the move, what does it mean to be the church?' To address that urgent question, he invites us to turn to the pages of the Bible, pages that are full of stories of migrants, refugees, and exiles. Carroll expertly guides us through these rich and complex narratives and carefully explains Old Testament legislation about how people on the move are to be treated. In these difficult times of ours, when so many have turned to the Bible to support unjust laws, policies, and practices that oppress and discriminate against people on the move, this vitally important book belongs in the hands of everyone who wants to understand what the Bible *really* says about migration and how Christians are called by our faith to respond with compassion to these brothers and sisters of ours."

—Jean-Pierre M. Ruiz, St. John's University, New York

"Carroll's *The Bible and Borders* is the best available treatment of how Christians should feel, think, and act concerning the issue of immigration. In a remarkably concise way, Carroll offers key biblical considerations relevant to Christian engagement with immigration—and immigrants. This is the book that needs to be in every Christian's hands right now."

—David P. Gushee, Center for Theology and Public Life, Mercer University

"In this deeply personal yet intellectually rigorous book, Carroll argues that the entire tenor of the Bible calls for a generous approach to human immigration. This book does not shy away from the challenges facing nation-states or their citizens, nor does it seek simple answers. Yet its meticulous analysis of the biblical witness underscores Scripture's clear call to regard all humans as made in God's image, subject to God's mercy, and therefore of concern to Christians of every stripe. This volume is a must-read for everyone paying attention to one of the greatest human phenomena of our times. Carroll appeals to our humanity and our faith, inviting a similarly hospitable response."

—**Mark W. Hamilton**, Abilene Christian University

"Immigration, and even the question of how we describe immigrants, is an issue that Christians cannot ignore. In this clear and passionate study, Carroll addresses this theme, showing how important it is across the whole Bible. Anyone interested in how we deal with this important issue will be challenged to think, and to pray, about this vital topic."

—**David G. Firth**, Trinity College Bristol
and University of the Free State

"Carroll is the rare scholar who not only interprets biblical texts in their ancient cultural contexts with profound exegetical insight but also applies them with prophetic vision to today's world. I was already using his *Christians at the Border* in the classroom. It remains a pioneering book that explores the ethical terrain concerning what the Bible teaches us about welcoming the immigrant as a Christian imperative and integral part of the church's ministry. This sequel builds stronger roads for the church to sojourn together. It makes the connections between the biblical texts and a theology of God's concern for the poor, the widow, the orphan, and the immigrant clearer, and with that clarity he issues a powerful challenge to practice hospitality and justice that only the most hardened soul could ignore. Read this book, but only if you are willing for God to change you. It can only be read as a prophetic call to action!"

—**Max Lee**, North Park Theological Seminary

The Bible and Borders

The Bible and Borders

Hearing God's Word on Immigration

M. Daniel Carroll R.

Brazos **Press**

a division of Baker Publishing Group
Grand Rapids, Michigan

© 2020 by M. Daniel Carroll R.

Published by Brazos Press
a division of Baker Publishing Group
PO Box 6287, Grand Rapids, MI 49516-6287
www.brazospress.com

Portions of this book previously appeared in 2013 in slightly different form in *Christians at the Border: Immigration, the Church, and the Bible*, second edition by Brazos Press.

Printed in the United States of America

Library of Congress Cataloging-in-Publication Data
Names: Carroll R., M. Daniel, author.
Title: The Bible and borders : hearing God's word on immigration / M. Daniel Carroll R.
Description: Grand Rapids, Michigan : Brazos Press, [2020] | Revision and expansion of Christians at the border.
Identifiers: LCCN 2019052622 | ISBN 9781587434457 (paperback) | ISBN 9781587434914
Subjects: LCSH: Emigration and immigration in the Bible. | Emigration and Immigration—Religious aspects—Christianity.
Classification: LCC BS680.E38 C365 2020 | DDC 261.8/38—dc23
LC record available at https://lccn.loc.gov/2019052622

ISBN: 978-1-58743-491-4 (casebound)

Baker Publishing Group publications use paper produced from sustainable forestry practices and post-consumer waste whenever possible.

Si la visa universal se extiende el día en que
    nacemos
Y caduca en la muerte, ¿por qué te persiguen
    mojado
Si el cónsul de los cielos ya te dio permiso?

Ricardo Arjona, "El Mojado"

For the LORD your God is God of gods and Lord
of lords, the great God, mighty and awesome, who
shows no partiality and takes no bribes. He defends
the cause of the fatherless and the widow, and loves
the foreigner residing among you, giving them food
and clothing. And you are to love those who are foreigners, for you yourselves were foreigners in Egypt.

Deuteronomy 10:17–19

Contents

Contents

Acknowledgments

This book has been percolating in my heart and mind for some time. Over a decade ago, Baker Academic published my *Christians at the Border: Immigration, the Church, and the Bible* (2008). Because of its ongoing relevance, a revised edition appeared five years later under the Brazos imprint. Across these many years, I have spoken on the Bible and immigration in a variety of church and denominational settings, on a number of university and seminary campuses, and at academic conferences. I continue to write on these matters for magazines and journals and to contribute essays to edited volumes.

These experiences, the amazing people I have encountered in these venues, and ongoing study serve as a continuing education for me. The desire to offer more than what is available in *Christians at the Border* led to the idea of this new publication, *The Bible and Borders*. The goal was to pull out the three biblical chapters from the earlier book and to update and expand that material. This volume is the fruit of that effort. Other recent publications present the personal stories of migrants, rehearse the history of US immigration and immigration law, and offer possible policy solutions. I addressed these issues to some degree in *Christians at the Border*, particularly as they pertained to the Hispanic community, but that is not the case here. This book concentrates on what the Bible can teach us about migration and those on the move.

My friend Jim Kinney, executive vice president of academic publishing at Baker Publishing Group, has walked with me in this journey of writing on immigration and the Bible, and for that I am grateful. With his usual kind and listening ear, Jim has engaged my passionate call about a substantive study of the biblical material for both the host culture and immigrants, and he has facilitated a platform for that voice to be heard. *Muchas gracias, hermano, por tu apoyo y confianza.*

Wheaton College has been a wonderful incubator for this book. The institution's academic excellence, its willingness to grapple with the pressing issues of the day from our faith commitment, and the daily stimulation of amazing colleagues are an encouragement to pursue the biblical perspective that is the foundation of this volume. Our Latino and Latina students (and the broader college community) are asking timely questions about immigration and the nature and mission of the Christian church, even as they wrestle with their cultural and ethnic identities and social responsibilities as a vibrant minority. I could not be in a better place to process these matters.

As I stated in *Christians at the Border*, I am indebted to my family. My mother, Edit Rodas Carroll, worked hard to plant in the deepest part of my being an appreciation for and the joy of *nuestra guatemalidad*, and my American-born father encouraged that. My wife, Joan, has journeyed with this hybrid of mixed heritage for over forty years. She has listened to our music, embraced our customs and food, and loved my Guatemalan family. *Querida, eres el amor de mi vida.* Guatemala is embedded, too, in the hearts of our sons, Matthew and Adam—another gift from God.

My prayer is that this volume might help all of us to perceive God's heart for the vulnerable and what such compassion means for Christian mission. I also hope that *mi gente tome confianza y consuelo en la verdad de que nuestro Dios nos acompaña en este largo y difícil perigrinaje de la inmigración. Su Palabra es nuestro pan de cada día.*

Introduction

The numbers on migration are staggering. The office of the United Nations High Commissioner for Refugees publishes up-to-date data and tracks monthly trends concerning the numbers and needs of refugees around the globe.[1] Other organizations provide statistics for the total number of people on the move (both within and across international borders), the percentages of those who are foreign-born in host countries, the impact of gender and human trafficking, and more. The International Organization for Migration, drawing from United Nations data, puts the total number of international migrants in mid-2019 at over 270 million.[2] Still other resources are more regionally focused, such as those that concentrate on the situation in the United States.[3] The magnitude of realities connected to migration—economics, health care, education, local and national security, cultural and demographic changes, and more—and their corresponding legislative challenges now dominate political debates around the world. Human history always has been characterized by migration, but at no time on this scale.

These tectonic changes raise questions for Christians. In a world where over 270 million people are on the move, what does it mean to be the church? What does the weight of this human need mean for Christian mission? How might all of this impact what it means to be a Christian today?

1

Even as more universities launch programs to study immigration law and migration and refugee matters, as the academic fields of diaspora studies and related fields flourish, as significant journals and other resources appear, and as the media do investigative reporting and present the human face of these dilemmas, the Christian church worldwide is responding. Church bodies are producing official documents to establish theological frameworks for processing these phenomena and to offer pastoral guidelines.[4] Theologians of various Christian traditions are doing the requisite historical work and careful reflection to address these issues.[5] Biblical scholars from various latitudes are looking afresh at the Scripture to gain insights into God's heart for migrants.[6]

This volume seeks to contribute to these Christian efforts. In the broader treatment of an earlier book, *Christians at the Border: Immigration, the Church, and the Bible*, I prefaced the biblical discussion with a survey of the development and current state of immigration law in the United States, relevant economic questions, and the history of Hispanic immigration.[7] Today others are treating those technical matters, and the heart-wrenching tragedies related to migration are being brought to light more and more through print and visual media. Accordingly, this book limits its gaze to the biblical material. It will explore the surprising amount of the Scriptures that reflect migration experiences and the Bible's teaching on dealing with outsiders. Truly, migration permeates the entire canon. My hope is that the native-born Christian will be able to better appreciate how central the topic of migration is to our faith. My desire, too, is that Christians who are immigrants, refugees, and asylees will find encouragement in the truth that they are dear to God.

Defining Terms

Serious consideration of migration matters requires becoming acquainted with an array of potentially unfamiliar terms. At this juncture, I mention only a few of the most basic categories.[8]

Other terms will surface in the course of the biblical exposition. To begin, it is important to distinguish between the terms *refugee*, *asylee*, and *immigrant*.

Refugees are persons who have fled their country of origin (1) out of fear of persecution because of their race, religion, social standing, or political views; (2) to escape an armed conflict; or (3) because of an ecological disaster (such as prolonged drought or a devastating hurricane).

For example, due to the brutality of the civil wars in Central America from the 1970s to the 1990s and now because of drug and gang violence, large numbers from those nations have sought asylum or refugee status in the United States, Canada, Europe, and Australia. Other major sources of refugees looking for a new home are Africa and the Middle East. Millions are fleeing hostilities from countries such as the Sudan, Congo, Syria, Iraq, and Afghanistan. The massive flooding and infrastructure damage due to record hurricane winds and rain in Haiti and elsewhere are increasingly motivating factors for migration of large population groups. In Africa and the Middle East, millions now are housed in large camps, where they can be confined for years, waiting for sanctuary. The United Nations coordinates aid to these camps and tries to place these refugees in host countries through its Office of the High Commissioner for Refugees. The number of refugees who can be resettled is governed by agreements with each of these host countries, which dictate how many they will accept each year. In the United States, once a refugee arrives, the government works with other agencies (often religious organizations) to help integrate them into their assigned communities.

Whereas the refugee process is directed by the United Nations, *asylees* present themselves at international borders and ask for permission to enter for their protection and well-being. Each country has its own profile of who can qualify for asylum. *Immigrants*, in contrast, are those who of their own volition move to another country for any of a host of reasons and usually petition for lengthy or permanent residence. Immigrants can enter legally—through official ports of entry and according to the rules of the admissions policies established by the host country—or not. Those who have come into the United States by other means are frequently called illegal aliens.

I prefer the word *undocumented* (or *unauthorized*) rather than *illegal* for several reasons. *Illegal* can have a pejorative connotation, suggesting by definition that the person is guilty of some act, has few scruples, and is prone to civil disobedience. This is not the case, of course, with the overwhelming majority of immigrants. Most would gladly regularize their status with the government, but the existing system simply does not provide appropriate avenues to do so. What these people have lacked is the proper documentation required by Washington and the workplace. They are not criminals. At the same time, the common label *alien* can evoke the sense of someone unchangeably foreign and other, without hope of reconciliation or mediation. In English, *alien* also is used for creatures from outer space, for nonhumans! Thus, the term *illegal aliens* is unhelpfully prejudicial. *Undocumented immigrants* is a better label to represent the current reality.

Other relevant terms for this book are *Hispanic* and *Latino* and *Latina*.[9] The word *Hispanic* originally comes from *Hispania*, an ancient name for the Iberian Peninsula. In more formal Spanish, *hispano* can still refer to things related to Spain. For example, Latin America (Mexico, Central and South America) is also called *Hispanoamérica*. The term *Hispanic* came into common parlance in the United States as a category designation of the Census Bureau for people of Spanish or Latin American descent. *Hispanic* is the word most people are familiar with and is regularly used in the media. Problematically, this very broad category lumps together those from many different countries, races, national histories, and even languages. For this reason, many academics and activists eschew the term as too imprecise and an unjust government imposition. They prefer the term *Latino* (feminine *Latina*). I certainly echo this concern, but in this book I will use *Hispanic* and *Latino/Latina* interchangeably because of common usage.

How I Came to This Discussion

My involvement with speaking and writing on the Bible and immigration stretches back over a decade. This engagement has very personal roots. I am the son of a Guatemalan mother and an American father. I was born and raised in Houston, but our family was very intentional that our home would be bilingual and bicultural.

I grew up speaking both English and Spanish, enjoying piñatas at our birthday parties, and celebrating *noche buena* (Christmas Eve) with Guatemalan tamales and black beans. Family and friends from Guatemala often stayed in our home, and my parents developed friendships with Cubans in the Houston area (my brother married a Cuban woman). Summers were spent in Guatemala, and during those times we got to know that wonderful country intimately and participated in Latin American culture in many ways.

From the early 1960s until December 1996, Guatemala was in civil war, and the rest of the Central American isthmus was in turmoil as well. My wife and I moved to Guatemala in August 1982, amid that fascinating yet tragic time. We raised our family in Guatemala City, where I taught Old Testament at El Seminario Teológico Centroamericano (SETECA). After fifteen years, we returned to the United States to assume a similar position at a seminary. Several years ago, we moved to "Chicagoland" and Wheaton College. During all this time, I have continued as an adjunct at SETECA and periodically return to Guatemala to teach and to spend time with family and friends.

That terrible war, which lasted over thirty years, and the current drug-related violence have generated a sizeable migration to the United States and elsewhere. Of course, many thousands from other countries have sought to come too. Today millions of undocumented individuals live in our communities, working and raising their families.

In many ways, I stand between the majority culture and Hispanic culture and can move comfortably between both. I must admit, though, that my deepest roots lie in my Guatemalan background. This is the primary impetus behind my interest in immigration reform, my experiences in Latino churches, and my work in Hispanic higher education. It also explains the motivation for my research on the Bible and immigration and for my accepting invitations to speak and write on the topic. Immigration realities play an important role in Latino and Latina biblical reflections because of their impact on identity and other sociocultural and political concerns.[10] So, when I am asked why I do what I do on behalf of Hispanic immigrants and why I study immigration, the answer is simple: *porque son mi gente* (because they are my people).

The Purpose of This Book

Immigration is a massively complex issue that has any number of facets and dimensions.[11] This book deals with one slice of the larger discussion: the scriptural basis for an informed Christian perspective. A better grasp of the amazingly rich contribution of the Bible to the national and global discussion can spur us all to seek a deeper wisdom that lies beyond the purview of the national media and political positioning. The goal of this book is to offer a solid foundation for a truly self-confessing Christian perspective on immigration.

Chapters 1 and 2 present the pertinent material in the Old Testament. Chapter 1 argues that the most appropriate starting point for approaching immigration biblically is the concept of the image of God. This is followed by a look at the many accounts of migration in the Old Testament. Chapter 2 explores the theme of hospitality in the ancient world and the Old Testament and then turns to the impressive legislation in the Law

6

(Pentateuch) dealing with outsiders. Chapter 3 attends to the New Testament: the life and teaching of Jesus and the concept that all Christians are sojourners in the world. I return to the matter of hospitality in the New Testament and close with observations on Romans 13, a passage to which those who are less open to immigration often turn. Each biblical discussion is followed by a section titled "Implications for Today." These are designed to stimulate thinking about how the biblical material might speak to contemporary realities.

1

"My Father Was a Wandering Aramean"

Stories of Migration in the Old Testament

How we see the world determines the values we hold, our understanding of life, and thus our attitudes and actions. Let me illustrate this with a mundane example. I have poor eyesight. For many years I wore bifocals. I cannot see either close up or far away without help. The computer age complicated my situation. For a while I had a separate pair of eyeglasses for working with my laptop, because the screen sits in that intermediate space that neither part of the bifocals handled well. Now I use progressive lenses. What is worse, if I want to read the small print on a label, I have to take off my glasses altogether and bring the writing up close to make out the words! Without my glasses I can still see—even if everything is a bit blurred. I am not blind. Once I put on my glasses, things become clear.

In a similar way, each one of us has an individualized set of lenses through which we interpret the reality in which we live and our identity and role in that context. These lenses are calibrated according to our background and experiences. For the Christian, the Bible can serve as a unique and fresh set of lenses. As the Word of God, it should profoundly shape our vision of life. The Bible is the set of lenses that brings us and everything around us into focus as God would want us to perceive it. This view of the world may be at odds with the way others interpret life, but the important point is that through the Bible we as believers gain proper perspective—the angle that God desires us to have on important issues.

In this book I present what the Bible has to say about matters related to immigration. This information can be part of the lenses that enable Christians—both those of the majority culture and those who are sojourners here—to process issues related to immigration in the United States today. This survey is not exhaustive, nor is it a technical exercise in biblical scholarship.[1] My goal is to demonstrate the breadth of relevant material in the Bible as a reminder that God has much to teach all of us on these issues.

This overview of what the Bible has to say about immigration begins at the beginning, in the book of Genesis, with the creation of man and woman in the image of God. What it means to be a human must be the foundation for any conversation about immigration. I then go on to discuss the many people of God in the Old Testament who, for all kinds of reasons, had to leave their homeland and settle somewhere else. Migration is not a new phenomenon; it is as old as time.

The Image of God

Genesis 1

Above all else, immigration is the movement of *people* across borders. The bottom line in any discussion on immigration should be that it concerns humans: their worth, destiny, rights, and responsibilities. The Bible gives great prominence to the creation of humans. Their creation is the climax of the creation account in Genesis 1. It is the last step in the divine movement to organize the chaos and fill the emptiness of the earth (1:2). In the narrative, the first three days of creation involve dividing darkness from light; separating the land, water, and sky; and preparing the earth for habitation (1:3–13). On the fourth, fifth, and sixth days, God places celestial bodies in the heavens, fish in the sea, and birds in the sky (1:14–25). The final piece of his handiwork on that sixth day is the creation of man and woman (1:26–31).

Six times the text says that God saw what he had made and that it was "good" (1:4, 10, 12, 18, 21, 25). Everything is in its proper place and functioning as it should under the gracious sovereignty of the Creator. The scene teems with sanctified life. With the creation of humans, however, the text declares, "and it was *very* good" (1:31, emphasis added). Fittingly, this is the seventh occurrence of the term *good*. Seven is a special number in the Bible and regularly represents perfection. The qualifier "very good" and the number *seven* together emphasize that humans are the pinnacle of what God has made. They are special indeed.

What is unique, though, about humans? Verses 26 and 27 provide the answer: every person is made in "the image of God" (cf. 9:6). But what does it mean that humanity is created in the image of God? How might this truth inform the immigration debate?

There are three primary views as to what it means to be created in the image of God.[2] The first argues that the image concerns what humans *inherently are* or *possess*. The idea is that every person has a will, intellect, emotions, and a spiritual component, all of which distinguish a human from other creatures. Others take the position that the image should be considered *relationally*. According to this view, the only person who ever truly incarnated the image of God was Jesus (2 Cor. 4:4; Col. 1:15), because of his direct relationship with God the Father. Individuals who are reconciled to God through faith in Jesus can participate in the image and thus regain the relationship with God that was ruptured with the rebellion of Genesis 3.

A third perspective explains the concept of the image within its ancient Near Eastern context. Other cultures at the time believed that humans were created to serve the gods by fulfilling stipulated ritual obligations and providing them food and drink. However, the only individual whom people could consider to be in the image of the deity was the king; he was the gods' representative and intermediary on earth. Genesis 1–2, however, reveals the "democratization" of the divine image; every person is made in the image of God, not just a select and elite individual. Nor were humans created as slaves to satisfy the whims of the gods. The biblical God has no such needs. In fact, he created humans to share in his rule! As God's vice-regents, men and women have been created to exercise dominion (1:26, 28) and to care for the created order as co-laborers (2:15). This privilege and responsibility require wisdom and creativity, and God has equipped every human being for this great task. In contrast to the other two views regarding the image, this perspective highlights its *functional* dimension.

Each of these three perspectives has a biblical basis (although the last seems to be the one most in line with Gen. 1). In its own way, each perspective underscores the special value of all persons: what they intrinsically are, their potential relationship with the Creator, and their capacity as rulers. Everyone is made in God's image and therefore has a singular standing before God and in the world. This truth can help us understand at least one potential reason for why the Decalogue prohibits the making of images (Exod. 20:4–5; Deut. 5:8). God has already provided an image of himself in humanity! Through humans and in relationship with them, God is present and involved in creation and history. Not surprisingly, the psalmist declares his amazement at the special role that God has bestowed on humans (Ps. 8; cf. 144:3–4). Sadly, the first sin outside the garden of Eden is fratricide and disregard of the brother (Gen. 4:5–10; cf. 4:14b, 23–24). Humans are quick to accuse and exclude (even eliminate) others made in the image of God. This, too, is an intrinsic characteristic of humanity.[3]

There is one other phrase in the biblical text that might be relevant. In Genesis 1:28 humans are mandated to "fill the earth" (cf. 1:22). This happens as humanity moves across the planet. Perhaps migration is part of the human DNA! Migration, then, for whatever motive, forced or voluntary, for good or for ill, is an *expected* human phenomenon. In the United States, many people change where they live to seek a better neighborhood, a new job opportunity and economic stability or advancement, education, to be closer to family, to have a new start in life or relationships, or the like. They move across town or cross state lines. Americans are a mobile people! For less fortunate foreigners, these moves, which can be motivated by similar reasons, are more desperate and require crossing international borders.

Implications for Today

Value as persons. The creation of all persons in the image of God must be the most basic conviction for Christians as they approach the challenges of immigration today. Immigration should not be argued in the abstract because it is fundamentally about *immigrants*. Immigrants are humans, and as such they are made in God's image. Each and every one of those who have come to the United States is God's creation and is worthy of respect. Because immigrants are made in the divine image, they have an essential value and possess immense potential to contribute to society and to the common good through their presence and work.

Human rights and the image of God. If one takes what the Bible says in Genesis 1 seriously, as revelation from God, then what it communicates about humans becomes a divine claim on Christian attitudes and actions toward those who come to this country—irrespective of whether they are here with or without the documents the government might mandate. To turn away in a disinterested manner or to treat badly one made in the image of God is ultimately a violation against God. As a result, the topic of immigration at some level needs to be considered from a human rights perspective and not be defined solely in terms of national security, cultural identity, or economic impact. For example, from the standpoint of national security, the primary concern is to control the border. Those trying to enter the country in a manner not permitted by law, then, are categorized logically as (and reduced to) intruders to be kept out. In contrast, a human rights perspective has as its particular focus the needs and fate of the immigrants themselves. This perspective can enrich discussions on border matters. In fact, immigration has been treated as a human rights issue within legal theory and international law for quite some time.[4]

Human rights language raises red flags for some people. On occasion it has been used arbitrarily by some special interest groups, and this can make some people suspicious of any reference to human rights. Whatever the ideological basis of those organizations, the point here is a biblical one. Immigrants are made in the image of God. Believers must examine their hearts for possible contrary allegiances that may lead them to ignore this foundational understanding of all people and its inescapable relevance for the treatment of immigrants. Misconceptions also can arise from a tendency to generalize. For example, some assume that all Hispanic immigrants are the same. Yet they actually come from different countries, each with its own history, customs, food, and religious traditions; nor do all come from the same racial, social, economic, educational, or even linguistic backgrounds. An image-of-God perspective should lead to an appreciation of the cultural richness, worth, and potential of those arriving from somewhere else.

At the same time, each person of the majority, or host, culture is also made in the image of God. This fact can add an interesting element to attitudes toward those from other countries. In the Old Testament, God is portrayed as limitlessly compassionate, not only toward his own people (Exod. 34:6–7;

Joel 2:13) but also to those beyond the community of faith. In the book of Jonah, the prophet admits that the God of Israel is merciful even to the Assyrians, the cruelest empire of that time (Jon. 4:2; cf. Ps. 145:8–9). His grace knows no bounds (Jon. 4:11). One way those of the majority culture can reflect the divine image is to demonstrate that same compassion to others—in this case, to immigrants who have come to seek a better life or to escape the violence in their countries of origin. Citizens also can correlate their own "migrations" within this country with the very same desires that those from other places have for themselves and their families. Moving is what humans do.

It must be made clear at this juncture that this conviction does not imply that there should be no controls on immigration or no order at the country's borders and ports of entry. What the image-of-God premise does, though, is establish a basic mind-set from which one can formulate policy and evaluate pragmatic decisions that must be made in the many spheres of national life. It should also inform the tone of Christian participation in the national debate. Ultimately, immigration is about people. This is where the discussion should begin, not with disputes over legal status. Legality is a topic that certainly must be dealt with, yet it is not the place *to start* discussions of immigration. In fact, this new starting point of the image of God greatly affects the nature of any legislation that will be formulated. An appreciation of immigrants as people can lead to laws that are compassionate and empowering for the immigrant and for the common good, instead of laws that at bottom are exclusionary and largely punitive—perhaps even xenophobic.

Expectations of the image. This word about the image of God has important things to convey to immigrant believers as well. First, it can be an encouragement. For many reasons, immigrants can feel inferior. They may have less schooling, come from a more deprived economic background (or have left significant socioeconomic and cultural status to migrate), have a hard time learning English or speak what they do know with an accent, and be of a different skin color than those in their host neighborhoods. They may not know the laws or handle cultural cues well; many live with perpetual fear of the authorities and are intimidated by their new surroundings and negative stereotyping and reception. The fact that they are made in God's image should generate a more edifying appreciation about who they are and what they can become, about what they can add to their new context and to the well-being of their communities. Whatever their previous or present condition, they are valuable before God and, therefore, valuable to the United States.

Not surprisingly, this theme of the image of God and Hispanic identity and worth is a major topic in Hispanic theological writing. What these authors try to convey is that Latinos and Latinas have significance not only as humans in a general sense but also, importantly, as *Hispanic persons*. It is at this point that the theme of *mestizaje* comes into play theologically and pastorally.[5] Their ethnicity is no longer something to be ashamed of. *Mestizaje* can be embraced as a gift from God and is inseparable from being a valued human being, a unique person, one from a special people with a matchless history and culture. Immigrants have intrinsic dignity as humans and as Latinos and Latinas.

The image of God makes a claim on immigrants as well. The fact that immigrants are made in God's image should cause them to reflect on what divine expectations of them may be. Their divine endowment has profound implications for the way they develop their capabilities in education and at the workplace; it should impact how immigrants carry out their responsibilities as potential citizens, raise their families, work at their jobs, handle their money, and engage the world in which they now live. They are more than victims.[6] In addition, immigrants should also value the host country's people as made in God's image. It is easy to be critical of things American as a defensive reaction to prejudice or in order to extol the mores of their own cultures at the expense of other cultures. But that contradicts what they themselves seek: appreciation for their backgrounds and abilities. For immigrants, as for the host culture, being God's representative is both a *privilege* and a *responsibility*.

Through its instruction on the image of God, the Bible can mold the attitudes and actions of the majority culture and immigrant Christians. For those in the majority culture, it can yield fresh appreciation of the immigrants' value and promise; for the immigrants, its message is an encouragement to forge ahead and an exhortation to live well as God's representatives.

Experiences of the People of God

A second way in which the Old Testament can inform immigration discussions is through its accounts of the many people of God who moved across borders. These movements involved individuals, families, and large groups. Sometimes it was voluntary. In other cases, the move was forced by famine or war or personal threats. The Old Testament is full of stories of people on the move. This is not surprising. In many ways, human history is the history of migration. So, too, is the history of God's people.

Some might contend that the Bible does not present details of the lives of immigrants but rather of refugees or deportees; therefore, it is not appropriate to appeal to the Scriptures for a study on immigration per se. This observation may be true in a strictly technical sense with respect to some biblical passages. Nevertheless, it ignores the fact that not all the migrations recorded in the Old Testament were of refugees and deportees. This argument overlooks the reality that immigration is not only about the reasons and mechanics of the move *to* another place; it is also about life *in* that new setting. In this regard, there are lessons to be gleaned from the Old Testament regardless of *how* these persons understood themselves and how they lived outside of their land.

Others might object to the following survey by pointing out that the accounts of the Hebrew Bible describe the experiences of Israel (and Judah), not of any and all immigrants. A question that others ask me is whether I am seeking to equate all Hispanic immigrants with God's people. The answer is no—even though there is a large multitude of believers among those who come.

The purpose of presenting this material is twofold. First, these biblical passages demonstrate how central migrations are to much of the Old Testament. This awareness should alert us to how universal this phenomenon is, and it can impact our understanding of what these texts portray and teach us. Second, these accounts depict how migrant people responded to circumstances at that time. These responses are similar to what Hispanic (and all) immigrants go through today. The text, in other words, can make readers more sensitive to the immigrant population and the challenges they face.

In the end, these contentions against appealing to the Bible in the immigration discussion, although trying to be faithful to the biblical text, miss the important truth of God's concern for the vulnerable. God has a deep love for the needy and disenfranchised, whoever they are and whatever the cause of their situation. The Lord's mercy is not selective. God cares for each human being because each one is made in his image. The most fundamental tenet of the Christian faith is that God loved the entire world so much that he sent his son, Jesus, to die for all humanity (John 3:16). The Bible also teaches that God is sovereign and thus involved in the movements of all peoples (Amos 9:7; cf. Acts 17:26–28). This means that in some way God is present in the migrations we are witnessing worldwide.

What follows is organized under three general headings: *hunger*, *forced exile*, and *life as foreigners*. Classifying the biblical accounts in this way can lead to a better appreciation of the various reasons people in the Old Testament migrated and how they handled each situation.

Hunger

The book of Genesis recounts the stories of several migrations.[7] Abram (he will not be called Abraham until Gen. 17:5) and his extended family leave Ur of the Chaldeans at God's command and travel hundreds of miles to begin a new life in an unknown place (11:31). After a stay in Haran, Abram is called to Canaan, where God promises to make of him a great nation and that through him all the peoples of the earth would be blessed (12:1–3). In other words, Abram's call to be the conduit of divine blessing to the world begins with his migration.

This relocation did not signify that he and the other patriarchs would settle permanently in one place. For the most part, Abraham and his descendants lived a nomadic life, even in the promised land. The only property Abraham is said to have owned was the cave of Machpelah, which he buys from Ephron the Hittite in order to have a place to bury his wife Sarah (Gen. 23; cf. 49:29–33). Several times in Genesis the patriarchs are called "sojourners" or are said to "sojourn" in an area for a time: Abraham (17:8; 20:1; 21:34; 23:4; cf. 14:13), Isaac (35:27; 37:1), Jacob (28:4; 32:4 [32:5 MT]), and Jacob's sons (47:4, 9). God also reveals to Abraham in a dream that one day his offspring will be "strangers" for four hundred years in another land (15:13). Indeed, that period begins when Jacob, his sons, and their families move to Egypt at the end of Genesis. This initial itinerant experience so marked Israel's identity that it became a part of the confession spoken by the head of the household when presenting the firstfruits of the harvest to the Lord. Deuteronomy 26:5 begins, "My father was a wandering Aramean . . ." (cf. 1 Chron. 29:15; Ps. 39:12 [39:13 MT]).

Not too long after arriving in Canaan, Abram journeys to Egypt (Gen. 12:10–20). There is a severe famine in the land, and he and his family migrate there to seek food. The climatic conditions in that part of the world are precarious, and nomadic pastoralists can be particularly at risk. The patriarch abandons Canaan and looks for sustenance in Egypt. Because of the massive Nile River and the rich soil in the delta and along its banks, in ancient times Egypt was considered the breadbasket of the region. Egyptians continually had to deal with foreigners coming in during times of shortage, whether for short- or long-term stays. They called the neighboring Semitic-speaking people to the east, including those from Canaan, "Asiatics." Reactions to the Asiatics varied over time, depending on the sociopolitical and historical context.[8] Egypt established a series of forts on its eastern frontier to monitor and control their comings and goings.[9]

Abram is often criticized for presenting Sarai as his sister to the Egyptians. He is fearful for his life as he worries that Pharaoh will want to take her. Indeed, Abram and Sarai are related (20:12), but Abram's plan compromises his moral obligation to his wife and puts his faith into question. However, reading this passage with a migration lens can add another layer to what Abram and Sarai do.[10] A famine has triggered their migration, and Abram, as head of his household and clan, is responsible for feeding the individuals and animals under his care. A desperate situation leads to a desperate plan. After traveling such a long way in search of food, the only alternatives are to enact the deception or to turn around without hope and maybe lose the struggle to survive. As one involuntary migrant has been quoted as saying, "To be a refugee means to learn to lie."[11]

Sarai is willing to put herself in danger so that all can eat. These kinds of terrible quandaries continue to characterize border-crossing stories. Women are especially vulnerable in these situations, but they take what can be horrific risks for the good of their families. What we witness in Genesis 12 is Abram, the father of those who now believe and trust in God (Rom. 4; Gal. 3), scheming to cross a border to eat. This does not exonerate him, but maybe the precariousness of the situation can make the subterfuge more understandable. He repeats this maneuver when they come to Gerar, a territory of the Philistine king Abimelech (Gen. 20). In both cases, fear is a motivating factor. In other words, added to the threat of starvation is the anxiety of physical harm (12:12–13; 20:11). Theirs is a deep sense of vulnerability as migrants, which leads to this drastic negotiating ploy. Isaac also moves to Gerar in time of famine (Gen. 26:1, 6), and fear of death once again rears its head (26:7, 9, 11). Jacob sends his sons twice to Egypt to buy food in yet another time of shortage (41:57–42:6; 43:1–8). Their sense of helplessness is on display before the power that they perceive in Egypt (42:28; 43:11–12, 18–22; 44:13, 18, 33–34). Eventually Jacob, his sons, and their families migrate to Egypt. There, under Joseph's sponsorship and provision, they escape hunger (47:10–13; cf. Ps. 105:16).

Forced Exile

Joseph. In addition to cases of migration to other places in search of food and water, there are instances where individuals or groups are forced against their will to leave the land. In the book of Genesis, Joseph is sold by his brothers (several had wanted to kill him) to passing Midianite traders. These in turn take him to Egypt and sell him to Potiphar, an officer of Pharaoh (Gen. 37:25–28, 36; 39:1). This unfortunate immigrant, in a place not of his own choosing and far from his family, proves to be a loyal worker with high moral standards (39:2–6a). But Joseph's uprightness is of no avail: he is wrongly accused of attempting to molest his master's wife and is put in prison (39:6b–20). Whose word would the authorities believe? That of the wife of an important Egyptian, or that of a foreign-born servant? In jail, Joseph's integrity and wisdom are confirmed (39:21–23). With God's help, he is able to interpret the dreams of his fellow prisoners and, more importantly, of Pharaoh and give him advice concerning how he should act on them (41:14–36). Thoroughly impressed, Pharaoh releases Joseph and promotes him to be governor over Egypt, one of the most powerful nations in the world (41:37–41, 44). Then this immigrant ends up saving the nation from famine (41:46–49, 53–56; 47:13–26)! He embodies the mission of God's people to be a blessing to the peoples of the world (12:3).

Joseph accommodates himself to Egyptian life in a variety of ways. Obviously, he is conversant in the Egyptian language. When he is to be brought before Pharaoh, he shaves according to Egyptian custom (Gen. 41:14). The ceremonial promotion of Joseph also fits that context (41:42–43). He is given an Egyptian name (Zaphenath-paneah) and an Egyptian wife, with whom he has two sons (41:45, 50). Joseph adopts the dress and makeup commensurate with his social station to such an extent that his brothers do not recognize him (43:8; 45:1–15). Joseph observes another cultural convention when he serves them food: it was not permitted for Egyptians to eat with the Hebrews, so his brothers are served separately (43:32). In accordance with Egyptian practice, Joseph embalms his father, Jacob, upon his death (50:1–3a) and is himself embalmed when he dies (50:26).

Nevertheless, Joseph continues to maintain connections to his place of origin. It is noteworthy that he gives his sons Israelite names rather than Egyptian ones. These names clearly indicate that he has forgotten neither his God nor his home (41:45, 50–52). He uses the ruse of having a translator present when speaking to his brothers, but he understands them and later speaks with them (42:23–24). This immigrant, in other words, has not forgotten his mother tongue. He is what today we call bilingual. Apparently, he moves comfortably between both cultures—two very different worlds. Joseph, like many immigrants, is concerned about the welfare of his family back home and uses his government position and the goodwill he has garnered in his host country to secure the entry of his father and his brothers and their families into Egypt in a time of famine (41:57–42:5). This well-placed immigrant directs them to Goshen, in the fertile eastern Nile delta, so that he can provide for them (45:9–11; 46:28–30; 47:11–12), and Pharaoh offers them a generous welcome (45:18–20; 47:1–6). In an amazing scene, Joseph introduces Jacob to Pharaoh (47:7). What thoughts and emotions does Joseph, a foreigner so integrated into Egyptian life, have as he presents his father—a shepherd, the kind of person the Egyptians despise (43:32; 46:34)—to Pharaoh? Shame? Pride? Then the aged patriarch, a powerless immigrant seeking refuge and food, blesses the most powerful man on the earth (another surprise fulfillment of 12:3)! Joseph's deepest longings surface at the end of his life. Before his death, Joseph declares his desire to have his bones returned to his ancestral land (50:24–25; cf. Exod. 13:19; Josh. 24:32). The respect and affection Joseph has earned from the Egyptians is manifest at Pharaoh's reception of his family and as the Egyptians share Joseph's grief at Jacob's death (Gen. 50:3b–14). From archaeological reliefs and inscriptions, we learn that in this general time period Egypt assimilated foreigners into their economic, social, military, and political spheres.[12] Joseph is an illustration of this openness; at the same time, he is an example of the conflicted nature of many immigrants throughout the ages who are torn between two cultures—their home culture and that of the host country.

Daniel. Joseph is not the only person deported from his homeland who served in a high position in the government of the host country. Another is Daniel. He and three other promising young men were taken from Jerusalem by Nebuchadnezzar, king of Babylon (Dan. 1:1, 3–4a). Babylonian foreign policy entailed taking the best of the leadership from conquered territories and retraining them for the imperial bureaucracy. During his time in Babylon, Daniel served four kings of two empires: Nebuchadnezzar and Belshazzar of Babylon, and Darius and Cyrus of Persia (Dan. 1–6). Throughout his long tenure this immigrant statesman steadfastly maintained his faith in the Lord. On several occasions he and his friends were willing to sacrifice their lives rather than compromise their beliefs and thereby won praise for their God (2:47; 3:28–29; 4:34–37; 6:25–27).

Daniel and his friends, although powerless displaced people, nonetheless resist complete submission and absorption into their conqueror's world.[13] The first chapter of Daniel sets the scene. In ancient times, military defeat was understood not only as beating the opponent's army but also their god. Therefore, the sacking of Jerusalem and the removal of the vessels from the temple in Jerusalem to the house of Marduk, Babylon's patron and head of the pantheon of its gods, signaled (to the Babylonians) a devastating defeat for Yahweh, Judah's God (Dan. 1:2).

These four young men were from prominent families. They were smart and knowledgeable, but now they were to be re-educated to serve the empire (1:4b–5). They were to be taught Chaldean literature, which was largely religious and would have contradicted their own convictions. Daniel's ability to interpret visions and dreams was also connected to religious belief (1:17, 20; 2:10–11, 27–28). Finally, the new names given them marked them as property of the regime, yet these names had religious significance as well. The names of Daniel, Hananiah, Mishael, and Azariah are called theophoric names; that is, they explicitly include the particles *el* (God) or *yah* (an abbreviated form of Yahweh), which identified them as Jews. In contrast, the imposed names (Belteshazzar, Shadrach, Meshach, and Abednego) invoked Babylonian deities (1:6–7).

Daniel and his friends had lost everything. They had been removed from their homeland, and from Babylon they learned about its brutal devastation. They surely had lost family and friends in the war, and whatever social status they had enjoyed back home was gone. Now Babylon was trying to redefine their identity. Their names were changed, and an indoctrination program was beginning. How did they feel? Humiliated? Angry and resentful, since now they were being forced to attend to the empire that had destroyed their homes, families, and lives?

The counter-initiative the friends take involves the food rations (1:8–16). They have no room to negotiate their circumstances. They are political booty, with no power, in a setting that is redefining their existence; they cannot alter the imperial curriculum. The one space potentially available for them to control is their diet. We cannot be sure why these young men consider the Babylonian fare defiling, but at the very least it represents yet another aspect of their subordination to and dependence on Babylon. What can be missed is something anthropological studies underscore: food is central to how people distinguish who they are. One has only to look at the ethnic restaurants and grocery stores in immigrant communities or how American tourists look for McDonald's in other countries to recognize how integral food is to self-definition. It is a tangible way to establish cultural boundaries; in the case of Daniel and his three friends, the food experiment made a statement about their identity and trust in God. The empire could take away all that they had known, change their names, and ready them for service, but they were still Jews! Forced migration had not changed who they truly were. And at the end of the test period they graded better than the native-born elites (1:20)!

Another cultural marker is the friends' faithfulness to God. Shadrach, Meshach, and Abednego are willing to die in a fiery furnace rather than bow the knee to the golden image of Nebuchadnezzar (Dan. 3), and Daniel endures the mockery of his beliefs (Dan. 5:2–4) and the plotting of political rivals that lands him in the lions' den (Dan. 6). Their moments of victory in weakness are coupled with the visions of chapters 7–12 to communicate, against all appearances, that the God of these displaced young men rules the nations and human history.

The forcibly displaced and refugees. The biblical text describes the involuntary removal and the flight of many others from war zones, but repeatedly these people are not named. They are the masses who are helpless victims, suffering the cruelties of war after war.[14] As we read these accounts, we must be mindful that with armed conflict comes the death of thousands in battle and untold numbers of wounded (as well as the need for mass burials), hunger, epidemics, the destruction of infrastructures and homes, the interruption of agriculture (if not the ruination of arable soil), internal dislocation, and more. Of course, there also is war's unimaginable psychological trauma. In addition to all of this, part of the consequence of war in the ancient world was that many would be forcibly displaced to other lands. For them, this was the final step of subjugation to the invader. The biblical text does not provide details about the months-long trek by foot and cart over hundreds of miles to reach the assigned destinations in exile. Surely their misery was great. Some were able to avoid this wretched experience and fled across borders to safety with the little they could carry with them.

In an incursion into the Northern Kingdom of Israel during a wider military campaign in 734–732 BC, the Assyrian king Tiglath-pileser III reduced the size of the Israelites' territory and took thousands captive (2 Kings 15:29; cf. 1 Chron. 5:6, 26).[15] Samaria, Israel's capital, fell to the Assyrians in 722 and was attacked again in 720; thousands more were carried off (2 Kings 17:1–6, 23; 18:9–11). These deportees were sent to the Assyrian heartland between the Euphrates and Tigris rivers, and some were sent farther east to "the cities of the Medes," which was newly conquered territory. On occasion, the Assyrians practiced bidirectional displacement, in which defeated populations were removed and then replaced with peoples from other places. This policy was applied to the Northern Kingdom after its defeat (17:23–41). This ethnic, cultural, and linguistic mixing was designed to make rebellion in conquered areas more difficult by grouping together those from different cultural and religious backgrounds and languages. In 701, Sennacherib, another Assyrian king, laid siege to Jerusalem (2 Kings 18–19; Isa. 36–37). Even though he was unable to take the city, in his annals Sennacherib claims to have carried away many prisoners and a great deal of plundered goods.

In time, the Babylonian Empire succeeded the Assyrian Empire. In 605, when King Nebuchadnezzar of Babylon made Judah a vassal state to the empire, he took a select group from the nobility and well-to-do, including Daniel and his friends, to Babylon (Dan. 1:1–3). After putting Jerusalem under siege in 597 because of Judah's rebellion against the empire, Nebuchadnezzar deported thousands, including King Jehoiachin and the royal family (2 Kings 24:14–16). A decade later, in 586, the Babylonian forces returned once again to brutally punish Judah for rebelling. They besieged Jerusalem for almost two years, causing starvation within its walls. When they finally took the city, they burned down the temple and much of the city and dismantled its walls. What remained of the elite and many others were sent away (2 Kings 25:11, 21; 2 Chron. 36:18, 20; Jer. 52:27–31). After witnessing the slaughter of his sons, King Zedekiah had his eyes gouged out and then was taken to Babylon, never to be heard from again (2 Kings 25:6–7). More leaders, and perhaps others too, were executed (25:18–21). The impact of the siege and of the demolition of Jerusalem and its aftermath are shockingly clear in the anguished poetry of the book of Lamentations. If this suffering were not horrific enough, the prophet Obadiah condemns Edom's complicity in the sacking of the city and in turning over fleeing refugees to the Babylonians (Obad. 14). A smaller, final group of Judeans was carried away to Babylon in 582 (Jer. 52:30). Unlike the Assyrians, the Babylonians did not bring in new groups to replace the deported populations. What had been the kingdom of Judah became the Babylonian province of Yehud.

Escapees and asylees. In addition to the people forcefully removed by conquering armies, there are examples of individuals who ran away to another region to save their lives from the threat of death.[16] Several are prominent figures in biblical history. In modern parlance, some would be classified as internally displaced and others as asylees.

With the help of his mother, Rebekah, Jacob deceives his father Isaac into bestowing the desired blessing on him rather than his brother Esau (Gen. 27:1–42). To avoid Esau's revenge, Jacob is sent far north to extended family in Paddan-Aram (27:43–28:5). There he seeks protection from Laban (29:1–14). This kinsman, though, takes advantage of the vulnerable Jacob and manipulates the marriages to his daughters for his own financial benefit. After many years, Jacob tricks Laban and makes his way back to his home and family in Canaan (31:17–33:20).[17] Moses bolts from Egypt after killing a taskmaster (Exod. 2:11–14). He goes all the way to Midian, a land hundreds of miles away, east of Sinai and the Gulf of Aqaba. There Moses feels safe, and he settles among the Midianites for many years. He surely integrates into that community during that sojourn, learning their language and customs (note the respect he shows Jethro; Exod. 18). He marries Zipporah (2:15–22), but when they have a son, Moses names him Gershom, saying, "I have become a foreigner in a foreign land" (2:22). The boy's name is a wordplay on the Hebrew term *gēr* (foreigner, sojourner), a term that will be examined in the next chapter. Moses's time in Midian prepares him for the realities of the wilderness wandering that awaits the Israelites after they leave Egypt. But Moses's Egyptian roots were deep. He had grown up in Pharaoh's court; his name may be of Egyptian origin (a point of contention among scholars). Moses had been given an education worthy of his social standing (2:5–10; cf. Heb. 11:23–27).[18] His migrant experiences and elite training would be an important part of God's plan to free his people. In due course, his assimilation process moves in still another direction—from adopted Egyptian and Midianite contexts to his Israelite heritage. Moses needed the Egyptian, Midianite, and Israelite cultures (including their languages) to engage Pharaoh and his court and to fulfill his divine calling to guide his people to the promised land.

The Israelites' escape from Egypt would not be easy, nor did it go as well as it could have. In their desert trek to Sinai, these families with their few possessions and animals had to deal with thirst and hunger. The deep impact of Egyptian culture is evident in their pining for its food (Exod. 16:4–17:7; cf. Num. 11:4–8; 20:2–13; Ps. 78:15–20). Ironically, when under pressure and feeling hopeless, they forget why they left that land of servitude. Difficulty in the migration trek to a better place leads them to second-guess that decision of faith and necessity. Because they fail to trust in God's plan after hearing the spies' report (Num. 13–14), they must wander those dry regions for many years. Finally, as the people move through others' territories on the way to Canaan, they are met with suspicion and hostility (Num. 20–25; Deut. 2–3). In sum, the migration out of Egypt and into the desert took longer and was more difficult than they had imagined at the beginning.

Other asylees appear in the biblical account. For years, David is on the run to avoid Saul's rage (1 Sam. 19–26). Motivated by his own sense of personal danger, David feels the need to take his parents to safety across the Dead Sea to Moab, the land of his great-grandmother Ruth (22:3–4). For some time, David lives among the Philistines at Gath, out of Saul's reach (ch. 27; cf. 21:10–15). Years later, Jeroboam, the son of Nebat, must go down to Egypt to get away from Solomon, who seeks to kill him after Jeroboam receives a prophetic word from the prophet Ahijah that he will become king over ten of Israel's tribes (1 Kings 11:29–40; 12:2–3).

After announcing a three-year drought to Ahab (which brings a famine), the prophet Elijah hides from King Ahab by crossing the Jordan River to the brook Cherith (1 Kings 17:1–7). When the water there dries up, God tells him to go far to the northwest, to Zarephath, a town along the Phoenician coast (17:8–24). Later, Elijah meets Ahab through the mediation of Obadiah, one of the king's officials. Obadiah had hidden a hundred prophets from Queen Jezebel's murderous designs (18:13–14). After the miraculous event on Mount Carmel and the execution near there of the prophets of Baal, Elijah races south as fast as he can to get away from possible retaliation by Jezebel. He reaches Beersheba in Judah and continues into the wilderness for forty more days, eventually arriving at Mount Horeb (Sinai), where he hides in a cave (19:1–18).

Archaeological data suggest that there was a sudden surge in the population of the Southern Kingdom of Judah and in Jerusalem in the last quarter of the eighth century BC. This could very well have been the result of a major flow southward of refugees from Israel who were fleeing the devastating Assyrian onslaught.[19] Over a century later, Jeremiah and his scribe, Baruch, were taken to Egypt by those involved in the assassination of Gedaliah, the governor who had been appointed by the king of Babylon to rule over the region after Judah's demise. The conspirators and their followers feared the vengeance of the empire. Even though the prophet told them to trust the Lord and stay, they made the decision to take flight to Egypt and seek protection there (2 Kings 25:22–26; Jer. 40–44). Others had fled east to Moab and Ammon or south to Edom to escape the Babylonian invasion (Jer. 40:11).

Life as Foreigners

The Old Testament does more than provide accounts of several deportations to other lands and of the efforts of others to flee persecution or death; it also describes the lives of the people of God and their descendants who lived in those distant places: the stay in Egypt that led to the exodus, the exiles in Assyria and in Babylon, the flight to Egypt, and the continuing presence of Jews in Persia after other Jews returned to the land. Archaeological material sheds additional light on those realities.

Egypt before the exodus. The circumstances at the beginning of the book of Exodus are far removed from the days of Joseph. At that time, the Pharaoh had graciously allowed Jacob and his family to come to Egypt and had received them out of respect for Joseph (Gen. 47:1–12). Yet there are glimpses of prejudice in that narrative. Initially Joseph did not eat with his brothers because of this (43:32), and then the Israelites were directed to Goshen since the Egyptians found shepherds detestable (46:34). A few passages inform us that the Israelites were in Egypt for about four hundred years (15:13; cf. Acts 7:6). For an undisclosed time during that period, the Israelites enjoyed protection under Joseph and those who had known him. However, as the book of Exodus opens, they have been reduced to slavery (Exod. 1:8), working on royal building projects and in agriculture (1:11–14). Egypt became a byword for a land of cruel labor, an "iron furnace" of injustice, and their deliverance under Moses would be celebrated as one of God's greatest acts on their behalf (e.g., Num. 20:14–16; Deut. 4:20; 1 Kings 8:51; Jer. 11:4).

Pharaoh and the Egyptians benefited from the Israelites' toil, but they feared the surprising surge in their numbers. They were willing to take advantage of the cheap labor of this foreign people as long as they were "invisible." Once the population of Israelites increased, though, the Egyptians began to worry that the Israelites might endanger their national security by joining any enemy who might invade the land (Exod. 1:9–10, 12). There was some historical justification for this anxiety. Years before, the Hyksos, a people apparently from western Asia, entered Egypt and eventually took it over for a time. They were defeated and expelled around 1550 BC. The Egyptians were determined that history would not repeat itself. Drastic measures were employed to control Israel's population growth, to the point of decreeing state-sponsored infanticide to eliminate the baby boys (1:15–2:4).

But there was never any question of curtailing their labor. The Egyptian response to Israelite complaints and to what they perceived as insubordination was to make their work more difficult (Exod. 1:11, 13–14). Eventually they even demanded the same quota of bricks but without providing the requisite straw (5:6–21). Straw was needed to stabilize the mud bricks. This decision did not make good economic policy: the Israelites were building Egyptian buildings (official ones!) but nothing for themselves. One would expect the Egyptians to desire efficiency and the best quality of bricks for the construction projects, but prejudice and the dread of this different ethnic group overrode economic common sense. Life for the Israelites was hard and their overlords cruel. The biblical description agrees with extrabiblical evidence of Semites serving as slaves in ancient Egypt.[20]

The Israelite midwives are amazingly resilient and resourceful in the face of Egyptian mistreatment and violence. Because of their belief in God, these brave women go to extraordinary lengths to save the Israelite baby boys (Exod. 1:15–22). Moses's mother, Jochebed, and his sister, hoping against all hope in the compassion of Egyptian women, watch from a careful distance as Moses is picked up by Pharaoh's daughter, and miraculously Jochebed ends up being her son's nursemaid (2:1–9)! Moses's mother and sister risked being discovered and punished by the authorities for disobeying the order to eliminate the newborn sons. What an amazing gift for Moses's mother to be able to hold Moses again and nurse him! Yet how hard it must have been for Jochebed when the time came to turn over her little boy to be raised in Pharaoh's household (2:10), forever removed from his family to grow up among their oppressors!

As the Israelites' suffering continues and hopelessness grows, they desperately cry out to God. God hears and answers (Exod. 2:23–25; cf. 3:7–9). The structure of the narrative in Exodus is instructive. Before the lament of the people is recorded, Moses is placed in Midian (2:15–22), where he receives the revelation at the burning bush (3:1–10). The plan of God, in other words, has already been set in motion. Under Moses they will go to Canaan, where they can live as a free people in a new place that offers them a better life, in a "land flowing with milk and honey" (3:8, 17). There they will have their own homes and vineyards, blessings denied them as slaves (Deut. 6:11; Josh. 24:13).

Assyria. The Old Testament is silent about the fate of the Israelites who were taken by different Assyrian kings from the Northern Kingdom in 732, 722, and 720, and from Judah in 701. Their deportation is mentioned, but nothing about what happened to them is explained in the biblical text. Archaeologists, though, have discovered inscriptional data and reliefs that provide valuable information about the life of deportees in the Neo-Assyrian Empire.[21]

The Assyrian deportations of 732, 722, and 720 had as their destinations the regions of Halah, the river Habor, Gozan, and "the cities of the Medes" (2 Kings 17:6; 18:11). Assyrian administrative documents reveal that the fortunes of individuals and of families in Assyria were quite varied. Much depended on the skills that these persons might have had and what and where the particular needs of the empire were at that moment. Some troops and charioteers were absorbed into the imperial armies, which were in constant need of reinforcements for Assyria's far-flung military campaigns. Other deportees found their way into government positions, while some deportees apparently were merchants. Carpenters and smiths seem to have fared well too. Undoubtedly, some Israelites were used in the construction of Dūr-Šarrukīn (Khorsabad), Sargon II's new capital, in the Halah area. The less fortunate, who represented a large number, were conscripted into service as domestics, were assigned to work on state or temple-owned farms or to unskilled labor-intensive jobs on building projects, or were made to dig and repair irrigation canals.

Through all of this, some assimilation into the Assyrian context appears to have taken place. This process may have differed according to circumstances and social standing. That this occurred is evident by data suggesting that later generations took non-Israelite names. It would also have been necessary to acquire the language of their captors; intermarriage was inevitable. At the siege of Jerusalem, the Rabshakeh, one of the Assyrian officials, spoke Hebrew (2 Kings 18:26–27). How is it that a high-ranking Assyrian could speak the language of a small country on the periphery of the empire? He may very well have been an Israelite, perhaps one who had made his way up through the ranks or had grown up among the exiles and was now serving the empire.

Babylon. After holding Jehoiachin for thirty-seven years (2 Kings 24:8–12; 25:27–30), the Babylonians showed respect to this captured king of Judah.[22] In the ancient world, it was not uncommon for such kings to live in the national palace. They were viewed as living trophies, and their treatment depended on the good graces of the victorious monarch. Evidently the Babylonians considered Jehoiachin to be the last legitimate ruler of

Judah. Uncovered administrative documents substantiate the biblical account that Jehoiachin and his family received extra rations. Eventually Jehoiachin was released from prison. He was given a seat of honor at the table of King Awel-Marduk, Nebuchadnezzar's son, who provided Jehoiachin with new clothes and a stipend. Nothing is known of the rest of his life in exile. Daniel and his friends, whom we discussed earlier, were also exiles who had a significant place in the royal court, even though they had to deal with occasional intimidation.

For some recent arrivals in Babylon, the initial shock of exile was overwhelmingly negative. In Psalm 137 the exiles express pain over terrible loss, over the deaths of loved ones and thousands of others, and over the ruin of Jerusalem. They mourn the demolition of their king's palace, the symbol of the Davidic dynasty and hope of glory; they lament the destruction of the temple, the special place of God's dwelling and the center of their faith. They *need* to remember; they can never forget who they are or where they have come from (137:5–6)! Their plea to God is that *he* will remember what has been done to them (137:7). They express frustration and shame at being humiliated by their captors. This psalm is a veritable roller-coaster of emotions about their being so far from everything that had given meaning and order to their lives. The cruel mocking of what they held most dear triggers an angry cry to God for vengeance.

It is to be expected that there would be a range of reactions to being stripped of all possessions and taken into exile, differences regarding how long the exile would last, as well as diverse experiences of exile in various settings. In terms of the time frame, some hoped for a quick return. Jeremiah sent a letter to Babylon (perhaps the city of Babylon), telling the earlier groups of exiles (2 Kings 24) that their stay would be long and that there would be no return for at least seventy years (Jer. 29:1–23; cf. Dan. 9:1–2). A few prophets in Jerusalem and among the exiles, however, had announced a much shorter time away from the homeland and opposed Jeremiah's predictions (Jer. 28; 29:8–9, 24–32). They, too, in their own way, were processing theologically the events that had befallen Judah. History would prove Jeremiah right. There would be several returns spanning decades, and a good number would decide to remain in Babylon.

Jeremiah's letter is important for another reason. It counsels the exiles to invest in their new land. The destruction of Judah and their forced displacement did not mean that God had abandoned them or that life away from the land was meaningless. They were to build houses, plant gardens, marry and raise families, and pray for God's blessing on that place (29:5–7) until the time of their return (29:10–14). This was a call to accommodate themselves to their new context, even to pray for it, and to appreciate that its well-being would benefit them too (another echo of Gen. 12:3). These migrants needed to learn that their current situation did not define them and that, despite their powerlessness, they could be instruments of God within the very empire that had conquered them! They must not see themselves as victims but instead as builders of a new future under the sovereign hand of God. Even if Jeremiah's mandate is understood to refer to marriage within the Jewish community and not to Babylonians or others, the prophet's message is the same: the long sojourn within that foreign urban context could be constructive.

Not all of the exiles, however, lived in that cosmopolitan metropolis. Ezekiel, for instance, ministered to those in a rural area, at Tel-abib by the Chebar canal, in the region of Nippur in central Babylonia (Ezek. 1:1–2; 3:15).[23] These Judeans would have been resettled there to work on the canal system or to farm land that the Babylonians were trying to make agriculturally viable. They would have been allotted land to cultivate (this also might be the setting for Jer. 29), but this would have carried the responsibility to pay taxes and render periodic service to the crown as unpaid workers on state building projects or in the military (a land-for-service system). In such instances, Babylonian policy was to plant somewhat homogeneous communities of similar national origin in the same place. Records mention the town of āl-Yaḫudu (literally, "City of Judah"), which indicates that most of its residents were exiles from Judah. Of course, exiles lived in other locations as well (another prominent place name is Bīt-Našar); the book of Ezra names several (Ezra 2:59; 8:15–20). The fact that elders were functioning within the exilic community indicates that the people enjoyed some level of autonomy in their daily lives (e.g., Ezek. 8:1; 14:1; 20:1). These settings in the countryside, where many of the exiles undoubtedly lived, may have afforded less engagement with Babylonian cultural and socioeconomic life than what is envisioned in Jeremiah's letter, although archaeological evidence points to some legal and economic interaction. The data also reveal a level of economic success and social status of an enterprising few (see the discussion on Persia below).

A recent approach to the exile experience in Babylon explains the biblical material through a generational lens.[24] According to this perspective, successive generations of those in exile evaluated their circumstances differently and held dissimilar theological views. For example, a passage like Psalm 137 would reflect the visceral feelings of adults who went through the forced removal to Babylon after the conflicts of 597 and 586. The letter of Jeremiah 29, on the other hand, is said to be directed at what now would be called the 1.5 generation—that is, adolescents who accompanied their parents on that journey but now were thinking of ways to flourish in their new land. This interpretation of exilic realities raises several interesting issues: How might those of the 597 displacement have interacted with those who arrived later—that is, the ones who lived through the horrors of a devastating war and the destruction of Jerusalem in 586? By that time, those who had come earlier and under very different circumstances may have already adjusted to the Babylonian context to some degree. Could they understand their countrymen's trauma? How did the children and later descendants of each group engage one another? Did Jewish views on the exile and God shift over time? These are questions that we may never be able to answer. Attempts to connect passages with specific groups can be subjective, but these sorts of issues are common to migration patterns in history.

Egypt. An unknown number from Judah fled to Egypt after the fall of Jerusalem and the assassination of Babylon's chosen governor, Gedaliah (2 Kings 25:22–26; Jer. 40). The biblical text specifies the places in Egypt to which these refugees went: Migdol and Tahpanhes in northeastern Egypt, east of the Nile Delta; Memphis at the mouth of the Delta; and the land of Pathros, much further south on the Nile River in Upper Egypt (Jer. 44:1). Unfortunately, there is little information available about their lives. The prophet Jeremiah, who had been forced to accompany them, denounces this group for worshiping other gods, particularly the queen of heaven (a title applied to several female deities in antiquity).[25] There is evidence from over a century later of a Jewish garrison on the island of Elephantine in the Nile, the southernmost frontier post of the Persian Empire. Scholars debate whether these Jews were descendants of the refugees fleeing from the Babylonions or of other migrations.[26] For a variety of reasons, over the next few centuries the Jewish population in Egypt grew. In the third century BC, the Septuagint (the Greek translation of the Old Testament) would be produced there. Years later, Jesus and his family fled from the threat of Herod and found refuge in Egypt, probably in the Jewish community at Alexandria.

Return migration to Yehud. The hope of a return to the promised land burned in the hearts of many of the Jews in exile. The biblical text records three returns from Babylon to Yehud: the first under Sheshbazzar and Zerubbabel (Ezra 1–2; cf. 2 Chron. 36:23–24), another under Ezra (Ezra 7–8), and the last under Nehemiah (Neh. 2). The Persians defeated Babylon in 539 BC, and the new imperial order made return to the Jewish homeland possible. The famous Cyrus Cylinder celebrates the Persian king Cyrus's magnanimous gesture toward peoples taken captive by Babylon, encouraging them to go back to their lands and repair their gods' temples. The Jews took advantage of this opportunity. Shortly after Cyrus's decree, the first wave of exiles departed from Babylon with royal backing. They recognized the hand of God in this surprising turn of events (Ezra 1:1; 9:9; Neh. 2:8; Isa. 44:28–45:7, 13; 48:14–15). The prayers offered in the next two returns (Ezra 9; Neh. 9) underscore how profoundly these returning migrants believed that God was guiding their journey back according to his will.

This voluntary repatriation retraced, again on foot and in carts, the hundreds of miles that the unfortunate deportees had trodden years before; this time, though, Jews were traveling not as booty of defeat in war but as returning migrants eager to begin life again in their ancestral land. At the start, they focused on erecting a new temple in Jerusalem (Ezra 1:68; chs. 3–6; cf. Haggai; Zech. 4:8–10; 6:9–15). Decades later (458), Ezra led the second wave. His primary concern was to renew the people's commitment to the law of God (Ezra 7–10). Nehemiah left Babylon in 445 in response to the need to repair the walls of Jerusalem, which had lain in ruins since the destruction of 586. He, too, challenged his fellow Jews to live lives worthy of their calling as the people of God.

The dynamics of these initiatives were complex.[27] The details of scholarly debates lie beyond the purview of this book. Instead, I highlight two matters that are particularly relevant to discussions on migration.

The first is to notice the different roles that two well-known Jewish leaders had in exile and their relationships, as descendants of foreigners, to the host culture and government. On the one hand, Ezra was a priest, and he naturally held dearly to Jewish cultural-religious boundaries. Even the Persian authorities recognized him as a key religious figure (Ezra 7:1–12, 21, 25). Ezra gathers other Levites (8:15–20), calls for fasting and prayer for a safe journey (8:21–23), and commissions the priests to deliver the gold, silver, and valuable vessels to the temple in Jerusalem (8:24–34). Upon their arrival, offerings are made to God. All of this is a very priestly perspective on things! Ezra is happy to receive help for the journey from the Persian king

Artaxerxes I, but there is no sense that he desires integration into imperial life or politics. He concentrates on making sure that the people maintain what he believes is a proper Jewish religious and ethnic identity.

The case of Nehemiah is quite different. Nehemiah lived in Susa, one of Persia's capital cities, and held the prominent post of cupbearer to the king (Neh. 1:11). He would have had to master Persian customs and political protocols to be in that position. Nehemiah's duties would have included tasting the king's wine at every meal to make sure it was not poisoned. This required absolute loyalty, because daily he would need to put his life on the line. Still, Nehemiah maintained a strong bond to his ancestral land (1:1–4) and faith in God (1:5–11; 2:4–5). When Nehemiah looks troubled, Artaxerxes is worried that he is ill (no king wants a sick cupbearer!). Yet he has earned the king's deep trust. When Nehemiah explains the source of his sadness and his desire to go to Jerusalem, immediately he is given permission and the promise of support (2:1–8). Nehemiah oversees the completion of this enormous construction project and takes on the job of governor. After a time, he is recalled by the king to Susa (13:6), but then he again returns to Jerusalem. Nehemiah is impressively competent and decisive, and his allegiances extend to places that Ezra's did not—specifically, to the Persian crown.[28]

The second issue concerns complications related to return migration. The time lapse between the various deportations to exile and the first return was several decades, and for Ezra and Nehemiah more than a century. It is not surprising, then, that the biblical text describes conflict and political intrigue against erecting a new temple in Jerusalem (Ezra 4–6) and later against rebuilding the city's walls and Nehemiah's leadership (Neh. 4, 6). Scholars suggest various reasons for this opposition, but at this juncture it is enough to point out that none of the returns to the land went smoothly. Questions abounded. Who had the right to the property after the long absence? Was there rivalry between the leadership in the religious community that had not been taken away and the newly arrived leaders? Who were the legitimate priests? Were the genealogies designed to legitimate those who had returned? Were there various factions within the community with competing social, political, and economic agendas vis-à-vis the Persian authorities? Defining their identity as Jews would have been difficult. Those who returned were not the same people. They had seen the larger world and the great cities of its most powerful empire at the time. They had lived among other cultures and participated in different ways of life within a context very unlike that of Yehud. Going back to that land was a return to the same place, but the returnees and even that place called "home" had changed. The opposition they endured perhaps arose from competing aspirations of those who did not want to see their status quo changed by the returnees. There would have been suspicion and resentment toward the newly arrived. On the other hand, had the hopes of those arriving from exile been fulfilled, challenged, or even shattered?

One of the biggest social issues concerned the intermarriage of certain Jews with those of other ethnicities, and hence of other faiths. Both Ezra and Nehemiah faced this reality (Ezra 9–10; Neh. 13:23–30). Their actions against these individuals and families can appear harsh to modern sensibilities, yet however we might judge their decisions, we need to appreciate the moment.[29] The Old Testament records other cases of intermarriage (e.g., the patriarchs: Gen. 28:5; 38:2; 41:50; 46:10; Boaz to Ruth). This historical moment, however, raised unique challenges.

This was a fledgling Jewish community, one ruled by a foreign power and trying to survive amid all kinds of obstacles. The surrounding peoples had tried to hinder the creation of a Jewish society, and now some Jews had intermarried with them. These other peoples were different politically, socially, and culturally. Language is fundamental to a people's identity, so the loss of the mother tongue made this blending even more alarming (Neh. 13:24). Ultimately, the foundation of the concerns was religious. The Law and their faith defined their understanding of the world and what was an acceptable lifestyle as the people of God. To intermarry would compromise or deny the demands of Jewish faith. In such a chaotic setting, the Jewish leaders saw their ethno-religious identity as essential for establishing a coherent community.

In the ancient world, religion was central to shaping and sanctioning a society. Today we compartmentalize religion and make it largely a private or even secondary affair; if we are honest, we usually do not see its interconnections with all of life nor make it the defining factor of our identity. Thus it can be hard to appreciate the deep passions of the postexilic context.

On top of all these internal tensions was the looming presence of the empire. In that sense, the return did not mean existence as a free people. Scholars debate how much control the Persian central government exerted over the provinces. Apparently local populations were allowed a measure of autonomy (how much is debated) in matters of traditions, laws, and customs—as long as imperial directives were followed, taxes were paid, and political and military strategies were implemented. Ezra and Nehemiah acted largely independently, but both received official approval and material support for their returns (Ezra 7:11–28; Neh. 2:7–9). Of course, Nehemiah served the king. Some Jews were being driven into poverty by those taxes; one of Nehemiah's solutions was not to receive his due as governor (Neh. 5). Truly, the return migrations were complicated affairs at various levels.

Persia. A common misperception is that most of the Jews returned to the land when given the opportunity by Cyrus, but that was not the case. The book of Esther offers a case in point. The multiple returns also confirm that not everyone went back. In fact, there was a vibrant Jewish community in the region (for example, it produced the Babylonian Talmud) for centuries. It thrived there until the severe persecutions of the mid-twentieth century, when almost the entire Jewish population was forced to abandon Iraq, the modern state that occupies the area of ancient Babylon.[30] Archaeological evidence reveals the socioeconomic activities of several exiles and their descendants from the times of the initial return to the land in 539 until well into the fifth century BC.[31] Among the documents found at āl-Yaḫudu, the place cited earlier, are a series of transactions by a Judean entrepreneur by the name of Ahīqam, son of Rapā'-Yāma. Like his father, but far more successful, Ahīqam improved his social standing and wealth over time by trading in barley, silver, dates, and farm animals and by lending money. His primary business contacts were his compatriots, but they also extended to the city of Babylon. Another trove of documents details the business dealings of three generations of the Persian house of Marašû of Nippur. This family worked as creditors and brokers of land and animals in the land-for-service sector, and descendants of Judean exiles are mentioned as clients or witnesses in their business dealings. Obviously, some of those exiled were enmeshed in the Babylonian and then Persian economic world and did well (cf. Ezra 2:69; 8:30; Zech. 6:9–10). Others achieved appointments to local administrative positions. In sum, many of the exiles dug roots in foreign soil, never to go back to their ancestral land.

The story of Esther exemplifies this historical reality. The account is set in Susa during the reign of Ahasuerus (Xerxes I), at least a decade before Ezra leads the second return to Yehud. There is no inkling that either she or her kinsman Mordecai have given any thought of living anywhere else. Cultural accommodation percolates under the surface.[32] Even though Mordecai is a Jew of the tribe of Benjamin (2:5), his name might be connected to Marduk, the chief god of Babylon. Recent discoveries demonstrate that it was a common name, though, so no religious significance needs to be attached to it. The issue is to be aware that it is not an Israelite name. Perhaps he has two names, as does his relative Esther. Her Hebrew name is Hadassah (2:7); the name Esther is related to the Mesopotamian goddess Ishtar.

After the king's servants search the empire for beautiful young women, Esther is chosen to replace Queen Vashti and is assigned by the king to the royal harem (2:1–18). Not long afterward, while Mordecai is sitting at the "king's gate" (2:19, 21; cf. 3:2; 5:9, 13; 6:10, 12), an impressive structure that was the point of entry into the palace precincts,[33] he discovers a plot to assassinate the king (2:19–23). He reports this to Esther, who relays the information to the king on Mordecai's behalf. Was Mordecai's act out of loyalty and appreciation to the crown? Sitting in that place suggests that Mordecai could have been a prominent person in society or the government. Unlike everyone else in that location, however, Mordecai does not bow down to Haman as Haman passes by; he explains that he does not do so because he is a Jew (3:1–4).[34] This refusal triggers Haman's anger. His reaction to Mordecai escalates into stigmatizing everyone of Mordecai's ethnicity, and Haman secures a royal edict to exterminate this foreign people, the Jews (3:5–14).

Upon learning what has happened, Esther decides to act. Whatever faith Mordecai and Esther may have had is subtly communicated by his famous line, "And who knows but that you have come to your royal position for such a time as this?" (4:14). Esther calls all the Jews in Susa to a fast (4:15–16; cf. 4:3).[35] Mordecai's question hints at a trust in the sovereignty of the Lord; Esther's call for a fast is common religious practice. The words of Mordecai in 4:14 may be taken as prodding her to step forward to protect her people. Her initial silence about her ethnicity (2:10) turns into a courageous plan. Esther has learned the ways of the palace and how to manipulate the king by organizing fabulous feasts. The rest of the account presents the growing sense of her identity as an outsider and of her responsibility toward her fellow descendants of Jewish exiles. In the end, Esther reveals her Jewish background (8:5–6).

This population was spared (and a measure of revenge against their enemies was attained [9:5–17]). To this day, this event is commemorated with the Jewish festival of Purim (9:18–32). The book of Esther dramatizes, as do other books that present life in the exile (Ezra, Nehemiah, Ezekiel, Daniel), that the God of this displaced community is sovereign over all human empires and active in the lives of his people. Their God can be trusted, no matter what the circumstances or place.

Implications for Today

Realism and everyday life. The Old Testament is full of accounts of people on the move or who have settled in other places. Many reasons are given for these migrations—whether of individuals or of large groups, forced or voluntary—that span centuries. They are part of the very fabric of biblical history—*and ours.*

The Bible offers readers realistic scenes and situations and amazingly true-to-life characters. In these biblical books are found the same kinds of factors that always have pushed people to leave their homes and begin the trek to somewhere else. Like today, in ancient times migration was caused by ecological factors (famine and drought) and war. Some desperately fled armed conflicts (of which there were many) across borders to what they hoped might be safer spaces. Others were not so lucky; to the trauma of widespread death and massive destruction in terrible wars was added forced displacement to faraway places. Still other individuals ran from personal threats.

The Old Testament migration is not just about *those multiple moves* over the centuries; it is also about *the sojourns* in other lands. The text depicts the life and experiences of these displaced people across multiple generations. We read about the personal and systemic challenges and the toxic xenophobic opposition they faced as displaced people. Finally, we read about *return migration.* In other words, the Old Testament portrays for us a wide panorama of the various migration realities and patterns that we witness around the globe in the modern world.

Above all else, it must not be forgotten that these immigrants and refugees are *people*, individuals and families caught up in the trials and tribulations of the time, events that often are beyond their control. These are lives of vulnerable populations of a small country, which are set on a broader canvas of international politics, economic challenges, and military forces. These migrants, from Genesis through to the accounts of Ezra and Nehemiah in the land of Yehud, suffer tremendous loss. They are tested and discriminated against; they work to provide for their families; they worship the God of their ancestors and the God of their exile; they have different jobs, some not by their own choice. Others are gifted in extraordinary ways and rise to positions of authority and do marvelous things for the host country of their sojourn. Some long to go back to their homeland, while others choose to stay in their new context. Those who do go back find that things are complicated. All wrestle with how to coordinate their background and heritage with the culture that now surrounds them, how to deal with the inescapable tensions of a new language, how to cope with a different set of imposed customs, faith, politics, economics, and laws. These displaced people are flawed individuals too—imperfect in all kinds of ways.

The text records as well the reactions of host cultures to this alien presence. Some individuals are compassionate, while others are cruel and scheme to exploit them or even eliminate them (e.g., Pharaoh, Haman). An aspect of realism around the topic of immigration, then, is that suspicion and rejection toward immigrants, refugees, and asylees should come as no surprise. That probably should be expected, at least to some degree. Herein are examples of immigrants and host people, good and bad, to be followed or avoided. In sum, the text presents a human face to migration and migrants.

A lively theological space. The spectrum of migration experiences that we read about in the Old Testament certainly reveals the living faith of these people. On the one hand, we witness theological debates and questions about what God was doing amid their migration circumstances and would do one day on their behalf. For instance, many cried out to God in their misery in Egypt and doubted if their God (and Moses) could lead them out; in the desert, they complained about the lack of food and water and God's provision. In the exile, there were competing voices about how long their sojourn would be and how they should live in that space. Jeremiah had to contend with prophets who were offering different messages to his people. On the other hand, we witness courageous stands for God in foreign lands, profound and passionate prayers, and the efforts of prophets to orient their people. No matter where the people of God were geographically—the land of promise, Egypt, Assyria, Babylon—the Lord was there to accompany, sustain, and encourage them. Their God was not restricted to any one place. Perhaps one could say that God always migrated with his people; our God is a migrant God.

Those settings were in complex and contested times, but they were divinely enriched moments for profound reflection on life with God. Many abiding truths in Old Testament books that we turn to for preaching, counsel, and devotional insights are revealed within immigration circumstances to migrants. Being removed from the familiar proved to be a creative, generative space for thinking about God, life, the direction of history, and the nature of hope. These stories continue to speak, whatever our context.

Migration and mission. There is much we can learn about the Christian faith from immigrants, refugees, and asylees; their pilgrimage with God will have had a trajectory that is different from that of those who have not migrated. Abram, the father of the true faith, was chosen for the mission of being a blessing. That call required him to migrate hundreds of miles to a new land. He wandered most of the rest of his life and began the mission of being a blessing wherever God's people go. Abraham, Joseph, Daniel, and others were a blessing in the contexts where they found themselves *as foreigners.*

Migrants continue to bless their new contexts in multiple ways, whether in the workplace, in the new things they bring to enrich the host culture (food, sports, abilities), or in the relationships that they forge with others (friendships, neighborhood gatherings, marriage). In the chapter on the New Testament, we will point to the unique contributions of mobilized Christian migrants who come under the label of diaspora mission. In this country we witness the growing presence of independent and denominational immigrant churches, which is having a significant impact on American Christianity. This is a spiritual blessing that has come by the grace of God.

Analogous situations. For today's immigrants, refugees, and asylees, this Old Testament material can serve crucial ends. It has the potential to be a scriptural mirror, as it were, where they might see themselves and identify with the descriptions and the experiences of its characters. Although the correspondence is not one-to-one because of time and space, they can actually "live" the text's scenes because they have gone through similar experiences and have dealt with comparable emotions and obstacles. Many immigrants seek a "promised land" of a better existence, a "land of milk and honey." But the trek here (or to another place anywhere in the world) can be hard, and life upon arrival can be full of long hours of work with low pay, few benefits, and uncomfortable treatment and prejudice. Perhaps they have left one Egypt for another. Those of the majority culture sometimes fear the demographic changes, migrants' numbers, and their being different; even so, the majority culture needs their labor. In the worst-case scenario, what can develop is a "Haman effect": the desire to get rid of an entire people group, perhaps based on an unfortunate experience or misunderstanding.

The exile and the idea of Christians being strangers in a strange land has been picked up by nonmigrant believers as a metaphor for living in today's society. The current culture has increasingly given up its historic and broadly Christian framework and conventions; for many Christians, it has become today's Babylon, where the people of God live in exile. This perspective is communicated at popular levels but also in more serious academic publications designed for a broader public.

Multiple examples can be cited. I mention just one: the influential *Resident Aliens: Life in the Christian Colony*, by Stanley Hauerwas and William H. Willimon.[36] From the side of Old Testament studies, pride of place goes to Walter Brueggemann, who has used the exile metaphor many times to describe the current status of the church in North American society.[37]

For Christian immigrants, refugees, asylees, and their descendants, however, the marginalization is not metaphorical; it is a lived experience in many spheres of their lives. For instance, Latino and Latina theologians have emphasized the exile as an appropriate paradigm for understanding the Hispanic situation.[38] The United States is the place to which they literally moved from another land, and they sense the separation from their home country quite concretely. This is an exile not in the sense that they are here as refugees or deportees; it is an exile because conditions in their home country compelled them to leave. And so they arrive, for instance, from Mexico, Puerto Rico, Cuba, Guatemala, El Salvador, and elsewhere in the Americas. But it is not the same for another group of Hispanics. In contrast to those recent arrivals, they have been here as long as they can remember, and millions are second- or third-generation descendants of immigrants. Theirs is not a physical exile but rather an interior and sociocultural one.

The backgrounds and experiences of Latinos and Latinas are infinitely diverse, but for all, life here can be difficult. Like the people of the Bible, they wrestle with language, different ways of doing things, an unknown political system and set of laws, and marginalization. What is "home"? Where is it? Who are they? What might it mean to "seek the peace and prosperity of the city" (Jer. 29:7) today and in this place? What are the appropriate parameters of accommodation or integration to this country? Is assimilation desirable? How profound and expansive will be their emotional, familial, social, and economic investments? What of their heritage will be negotiated away "to fit in," and what will inevitably be lost over time as they go through the school system, into the job market, and engage the majority culture? That process will be different for each person and family (and for each immigrant group, as it has always been in our history). There is a wonderful title to a book in Spanish that captures this engagement between text and context so powerfully: *En la dispersión, el texto es patria* (In the diaspora, the text is the home country).[39] The Bible, in other words, is where Hispanics can find themselves and find God in their "exile."

If what immigrants see in the text is themselves, then—if that seeking is honest—what they also see are sinners and flawed people. It will not do to idealize their situation or culture; the Old Testament does not do this. Its realism reminds us that the movement of peoples is not tidy and that any group is a mixed lot.

In the Bible's richness, much is available for the majority culture and for migrants. To the former, it reveals that migration is a human condition to be appreciated and demands a response of grace. For those who are sojourners, there is much to ponder about life and faith. In the midst of all of that, we see immigrant believers doing what they can to fulfill their calling as the people of God to bless others.

Conclusion

This chapter has covered a lot of ground. It began with the theme of the image of God and what it means to be human. This must be the place where Christians begin discussions on immigration. The next major section rehearsed the many instances of migration in the Old Testament and pointed out their different causes. It also discussed the variety of cultural and faith responses of both migrants and host peoples.

The complicated picture in the text is startling. The situation today is complicated too! This is good news. The Bible is complex enough to connect with the realities of human life. Because its depictions are true to life, as the Word of God it can orient believers of the majority culture and immigrant communities about the proper attitudes and perspectives with which all sides should engage the national debate.

The next chapter continues the exploration of the Old Testament. First, it will locate the treatment of the immigrant within the general ethos of hospitality that was common in the ancient world. The second section deals with legislation concerning foreigners in Israel's law. Attitudes are important, but sooner or later societies must regulate themselves in concrete ways. It is no different in our world today.

2

"You Are to Love Those Who Are Foreigners"

Old Testament Law and the Sojourner

Give me your tired, your poor,
Your huddled masses yearning to breathe free,
The wretched refuse of your teeming shore.
Send these, the homeless, tempest-tost, to me,
I lift my lamp beside the golden door!

Many Americans recognize these lines. They come from a poem by Emma Lazarus titled "The New Colossus," which she wrote in 1883 to help raise money to construct the pedestal of the Statue of Liberty in New York harbor. The statue had been commissioned as a gift from the French government to the United States to commemorate the centennial of American independence in 1876, but it was not completed until 1886. It was not until 1903 that Lazarus's poem was engraved on a plaque and placed inside the pedestal.

Over the years, and not infrequently in the current debate, these lines have been used to claim that the Statue of Liberty stands as a powerful symbol of the fact that the United States is a nation of immigrants. Some dispute this view.[1] I will not contest the repudiation of the immigrant interpretation. It is enough to emphasize that, at the very least, this 130-year-old memorial and this poem communicate a charitable openness, an ethos of national hospitality to the vulnerable.

The preceding chapter was primarily concerned with the experiences *of* the people of God as sojourners; in this chapter the focus is on how outsiders are received *by* the people of God, both culturally and legally. The notion of generous hospitality toward others pervades the Old Testament. This chapter opens with a brief exploration of the ethics of hospitality in ancient Israel. The second section surveys Old Testament laws concerning foreigners, which are amazingly welcoming, especially in comparison with the rest of the ancient Near East.

In the end, the reception of immigrants, refugees, and asylees must be made concrete and formalized in legislation—that is, in laws that regulate entry and that stipulate their rights, benefits, and obligations. It is the contention of this chapter that Old Testament law offers moral principles for treatment of the outsider. Those principles were systematized in a suitable way for a certain time and place in the laws of Israel. Today's world is very different from the world in which they were applied. Therefore, it would make no sense to mimic those ancient law codes. The principles that were their foundation endure, however, and transcend that context. The fact that immigration matters are found in legislation means that the discussions cannot be limited to an array of personal matters; immigration has systemic dimensions, and it is on these systems that biblical principles need to have an impact.

Hospitality in the Ancient World

Old Testament Practices

Travel in Old Testament times could be treacherous. There were potential dangers to be faced on the road (such as robbery or a mishap), and there was the challenge en route of finding sufficient food and drink and a safe haven at night. The cultures across the ancient Near East responded to these needs with shared conventions of hospitality toward the stranger. There were protocols and expectations for the host to be openhanded and for visitors not to abuse their welcome. It was assumed, too, that this act of kindness would be reciprocated if the host journeyed to the guest's land.

Israel was not an exception to this widespread cultural ethic.[2] A notable example of this practice in the Old Testament is Abraham's interaction with the three strangers who appear at his tent in Genesis 18. The patriarch comes out to greet them and immediately offers them the best refreshment he can before they go on their way, not knowing that these visitors are divinely sent (cf. 2 Kings 4:8–10; Heb. 13:2). This event made quite an impression on ancient readers. First Clement, a letter from the church in Rome to the Christians at Corinth at the end of the first century, declares that Abraham was given a son because of his faith and this act of hospitality (1 Clement 10.6–7).[3]

Other scenes of liberal hospitality occur elsewhere in the Bible. In Genesis 24 Rebekah's brother Laban offers food to Abraham's servant and provision for his camels. In Exodus 2 the Midianite Reuel chastises his daughters for not inviting the "Egyptian" Moses to have something to eat. In 2 Kings 4 the prophet Elisha receives care from the Shunammite couple. How self-sacrificing this commitment to others could be is exemplified by the poor widow of Zarephath, who self-sacrificially is willing to share with the prophet Elijah what little she has left for herself and her son (1 Kings 17).

There are also cases where things go terribly wrong. The actions of the men of Sodom in Genesis 19 are an extreme departure from Abraham's charitableness. Lot, even though he himself is an outsider living in the town (19:9), welcomes into his home the visitors who earlier had been with Abraham (19:1–3). But when the situation gets out of control, he shockingly offers his daughters to the crowd to protect the strangers

(19:4–11). In the second half of Judges 19, the Levite refuses to try the hospitality of Jebus (that is, Jerusalem), because it was not an Israelite city. Instead, he and his concubine travel on to Gibeah of the tribe of Benjamin, with horrific consequences. Hospitality to the stranger is a virtue. Job cites his care of the sojourner and traveler as testimony to his integrity (Job 31:32), and in the book of Isaiah hospitality to the homeless is listed as proof of true faith in God (Isa. 58:6–7). Some interpreters understand Psalm 23 to allude to the custom of hospitality (v. 5). If this interpretation is correct, then graciousness toward the needy is revealed to be an attribute of God himself. It is no wonder that a charitable spirit and material sharing are to characterize the Lord's people. Whatever might have been the common cultural impulse to be gracious to the stranger in ancient times, it is here given a more profound motivation. To be hospitable is to imitate God.

Implications for Today

The host. In the United States, it can seem as if it is becoming more and more difficult to be hospitable, to take the time to be with others, and to welcome them into one's home. Life is so busy and full of activity. Families can be so fractured that few are able to slow down and open their hearts and hearths to anyone, let alone someone different. Nevertheless, clinging to a chosen lifestyle and schedule, defining the permitted parameters of a neighborhood, and monopolizing time just for oneself and one's family so that the stranger—any stranger—is excluded might be rebellion against God. The biblical challenge to be hospitable to the stranger is set before individual believers and Christian communities alike.

The theme of hospitality is relevant to the immigration debate. The biblical text can gently prod believers of the majority culture to a greater mind-set of hospitality and to actions of hospitality toward the strangers who are immigrants from Latin America and other places around the globe. To be sure, there are other strangers among the normal day-to-day contacts of the majority culture. These could be a visitor at church, a neighbor, or someone at work. But there is an immense group of other strangers with foreign roots who cannot be dismissed. What I am not doing here (and what I cannot do) is defining what shape that hospitality should take. It can take an infinite number of forms: from small gestures of greeting or sharing a meal, to broader-scale initiatives through a ministry or organization directed toward the specific needs of immigrants, to involvement in political activism at various levels. The key is having an attitude of hospitality, a gracious spirit, toward these strangers.

The recipient. The implications of the call to hospitality cannot be limited to the majority culture. Biblically, there is the expectation that the sojourner will not abuse the hospitality that is extended. Unfortunately (and not surprisingly), there are some cases of immigrants who take advantage of certain services and of well-meaning individuals for personal gain. There is also a criminal element within immigrant communities (as there is in any community of any race or ethnicity of native-born people!). This constitutes a small percentage within the immigrant population, but they are the ones to whom opponents of immigration point; they are the ones who appear on the nightly news and are wrongfully portrayed as the face of the entire immigrant population. In this country, where a portion of the majority culture can be nervous and skeptical, this negative element of immigrant communities must be acknowledged. At the same time, and more importantly, the appreciation of the greater part of immigrants toward the United States needs to be communicated to the wider culture. I have been in prayer meetings with Hispanic pastors and churches where, as a people of God, we have sent up prayers of thanksgiving for this country and for the opportunities it has afforded immigrants. This is the proper response of the beneficiary of hospitality, and it is pervasive among immigrant believers. Sadly, however, this gratitude can be mixed with fear and uncertainty because of experiences of prejudice or by what is broadcast on television and social media. Might not majority-culture Christians set an example in hospitable attitudes and actions toward the strangers among us? This could be a testimony of Christian faith and a genuine help and encouragement to those who have come to this country.

If hospitality is important in the Old Testament, it is fundamental to the message of the New Testament as well. We will return to this theme and its possible lessons for today in the next chapter.

Legislation concerning the Sojourner

Hospitality functions primarily on an informal basis at the personal and familial level. Its practice suggests that a people group has a spirit of being openhanded. A test of this possibility is to examine their laws and the structures of their society to ascertain whether the moral qualities of charitable welcome and kindness toward the outsider find expression in legislation and thus in socioeconomic and legal spaces. In other words, do these qualities impact how the society actually operates? What is more, does the treatment of the outsider reveal something about the soul of the host country?

Law in the Old Testament

Misunderstandings. Many Christians have a distorted view of Old Testament law. Based on a certain reading of some verses in the Pauline Epistles, they can hold to two erroneous presuppositions. First, for many, the Old Testament law essentially is about sacrifices that deal with sin and nothing more. This is wrong on several counts. Not all sacrifices concern forgiveness of sin (such as the grain and fellowship offerings in Lev. 2–3; 6:14–23; 7:11–26). In addition, as I discuss below, Israel's law codes touch many areas of life beyond religious rituals.

56

The second misunderstanding involves holding that Jews since the time of Moses (and especially in Jesus's day) believed that they had to obey the law in order to earn the right to be the people of God; in other words, theirs was a religion of works, while Christians, in contrast, are freed from the unforgiving legalism of that law and can proclaim that salvation is by grace through faith alone. This perspective also reveals a flawed notion of what the Old Testament law is and how it works. For a more correct appreciation, it is helpful to look at the narrative in which the law is given to Israel. The flow of that account makes it unmistakably plain that the law was never intended to provide a way for the nation to earn a relationship with God.

Narrative context of the giving of the law. In Exodus 19 the people of God under the guidance of Moses have come to a mountain in the desert of Sinai. There they receive a unique revelation from the Lord. When this happens, Israel has already celebrated the Passover in Egypt: their firstborn were spared divine judgment because blood of lambs had been put on the doorposts of their homes (Exod. 12). Then the people miraculously crossed the Red/Reed Sea and witnessed the defeat of Pharaoh's army (13:17–14:31). In other words, when the law is given to the nation through Moses, it is directed at a redeemed people. The law, therefore, was not designed to stipulate *how to achieve redemption*; rather, its purpose was to show them *how to live as a redeemed people.* Notice that the account begins with "You yourselves have seen what I did to Egypt, and how I carried you on eagles' wings and brought you to myself" (19:4). The prologue to the Ten Commandments underscores the established fact of their redemption: "I am the LORD your God, who brought you out of Egypt, out of the land of slavery" (20:2). The giving of the laws follows this assertion.

The narrative context for the giving of the law can be expanded beyond the preceding chapters in the book of Exodus. In the call of Abram in Genesis 12, the patriarch is told that he and his descendants will be the channel of God's blessing to the rest of the world (12:1–3). Centuries later, when the law is entrusted to Israel, it is presented in such a way as to communicate that the law itself and the society that it was to shape and regulate are to be a divine blessing. The key text is worth citing in full. Moses is speaking:

> See, I have taught you decrees and laws as the LORD my God commanded me, so that you may follow them in the land you are entering to take possession of it. Observe them carefully, for this will show your wisdom and understanding to the nations, who will hear about all these decrees and say, "Surely this great nation is a wise and understanding people." What other nation is so great as to have their gods near them the way the LORD our God is near us whenever we pray to him? And what other nation is so great as to have such righteous decrees and laws as this body of laws I am setting before you today? (Deut. 4:5–8)

The law and the nations. The content of the law and Israel's adherence to its statutes were designed to point the surrounding peoples to the greatness of God and his wisdom. But there is something more here. Christopher Wright uses the term *paradigm* to explain this other purpose of the law. He explains that these laws "constituted a concrete model, a practical, culturally specific, experimental exemplar of the beliefs and values they embodied."[4] Through the medium of the law and its incarnation in the nation, the moral demands of God would be visible in concrete ways in the multiple spheres of Israel's social life. The law was to offer the world of that time an example of what a life pleasing to God would look like. One area of the law prescribed to Israel is the attitude toward and treatment of the stranger.

The fact that this set of laws was to be a light to the nations does not mean, however, that it would be totally distinct from other ancient Near Eastern law codes. In fact, one should expect some degree of overlap between the laws of the Old Testament and the law collections of other cultures in that geographical area, as they confront similar issues. In fact, that is what we find. For one thing, these law codes deal with conventional social issues such as marriage, property rights and procedures for inheritance, loans, theft, and murder. Second, it is natural that the broadly shared cultural and historical milieu of Mesopotamia and Syro-Palestine would yield some commonalities in language and content.[5]

At the same time, there are important differences between Israelite law and these other collections. These differences are ultimately grounded in the character of the divine Lawgiver and in what he has done for his people. Recent studies demonstrate the dissimilarities, based on these two foundations, in such areas as the mercy shown to the poor and the political ideology of the monarchy.[6] This will also be apparent in our study of the treatment given to the foreigner.

One final pertinent observation remains to be made, and it comes from a discipline called interpretive anthropology.[7] Although most people do not perceive it in this way, interpretive anthropology teaches us that a system of law largely generates and is a reflection of a society's culture. In other words, what a particular culture defines as "true" and "right" in its legal principles and processes can actually be its own sociohistorical construct. It has a history; there are reasons why things are the way they are and function as they do. A society's law attempts to put all of life in its proper place, organize its chaos, and adjudicate its conflicts. How the law is structured, the kinds of privileges and protections it offers, the demands and limits it imposes, and the institutions it establishes—all of these reveal that society's values and priorities. The laws disclose what that society understands to be correct and good. A society's legal system, therefore, is a window into its heart.

This perspective adds another dimension to what we have been saying about Old Testament law. We should recognize that the way it deals with the foreigner says something very important about Israel's fundamental character and about the God who gave it these rules. Wright is correct that the law was to be a paradigm for the world. Interpretive anthropology would add the insight that it is not just that specific laws serve as a model for other nations. These laws also reflect something deeper: Israel's stance toward the foreigner was part of the larger fabric of its ethical life. It was an important part of the ethos of what it meant to be the people of God.

Terminology for the Sojourner

Nations of the ancient world were not construed in the same way as modern nation-states. Nonetheless, there clearly was a sense of territorial boundaries; that is, national borders are not a recent phenomenon.[8] Like today, these borders followed natural geographical or topographical lines (such as rivers and mountains) and could be formalized by treaty or imposed through war. On multiple occasions the biblical text mentions specific geographical areas connected to different peoples and to states of various sizes, such as the lands of Egypt, the Philistines, Edom, Moab, Ammon, and several city-states. Nations could protect their borders with patrols and forts to monitor incursions, peaceful or otherwise.

Israel is aware that it is crossing other peoples' territories on their journey to the promised land; they have a sense that, at some level, borders are established by God (Deut. 32:8–9; cf. Ps. 74:17; Acts 17:26). So the Israelites ask permission to pass through other lands but receive a negative response (Num. 20–24; Judg. 11:16–20). This is not surprising. As a large group, Israel would need to eat off the land or secure food from these peoples as it marched. Perhaps they also saw Israel as a military threat because of what they had heard about the exodus from Egypt. The promised land to which they travel is given limits (Num. 34:1–12; Deut. 11:24; cf. Gen. 15:18), and the territory of each of the twelve tribes is presented in detail (Josh. 13–19; cf. Deut. 3:12–17). The extent of the United Monarchy is cited several times (whether as an ideal or as what was truly under its control; e.g., 2 Sam. 3:10; 24:5–8; 1 Kings 4:25), and there were occasions when Israel had territorial disputes with neighboring nations. An example of this tension was the ongoing conflict with Aram (that is, Syria) over Ramoth Gilead to the northeast (e.g., 1 Kings 22:1–2; 2 Kings 9:1–5). In the gradual process of their defeats by Assyria and Babylon, the boundaries of the Northern Kingdom (Israel) and the Southern Kingdom (Judah) became smaller and smaller as they progressively were incorporated into those empires. After their final defeat, their national territories were reconfigured into imperial provinces. Borders mattered.

What is more, ancient peoples could distinguish themselves from those who came from somewhere else. They were aware of other languages, customs, attire, religions, and governments. They would have come into contact with traders, caravans, mercenaries, political exiles, and officials from other nations, as well as runaway slaves, refugees, and foreigner settlers. Perhaps they had witnessed foreign armies marching through their territory.

How were outsiders perceived and treated in the ancient Near East? Were these sentiments expressed in law or other legal and social arrangements? How did Israel react to outsiders who entered its land? The Old Testament contains a surprising amount of legislation dealing with outsiders. Some even suggest that concern for the stranger lies at the very heart of Old Testament law because of what it reveals about our God and about the kind of community God's people were (and are) supposed to be.[9] Were these laws welcoming and charitable, or were they exclusionary and punitive?

Several terms are used in the Old Testament to refer to outsiders. They are *gēr*, *tôšab*, *nokrî* (and the related *ben-nēkār*), and *zār*.[10] As we proceed, two comments are in order. First, English versions are not consistent in their translations. Sometimes the same English word is used for more than one of these Hebrew terms, and different English words may be used for the same one. In what follows, I will stay primarily with the transliteration of the Hebrew, but the translation options of some English versions will occasionally be mentioned. Second,

Old Testament legislation appears in several law codes, which have been given various names by scholars: the Ten Commandments or Ten Words (Exod. 20:1–17; Deut. 5:6–21), the Covenant Code (Exod. 21:1–23:33), the Holiness Code (Lev. 17–26 [or 17–27]), and the Deuteronomic Code (Deut. 12–26). Laws pertaining to foreigners also appear in the book of Numbers and in chapters in Deuteronomy that frame the law section (i.e., chs. 1–11, 27–32). Scholars observe varying considerations of the outsider between (and within) these codes, and some try to reconstruct what they postulate to be the possible historical sequence of their appearance.[11] This kind of approach has especially characterized studies of *gēr*, particularly in the book of Deuteronomy.[12] Our presentation, however, surveys this legal material as we now have it in our Bibles, but without highlighting distinctions between the law collections.[13] While there are differing nuances among them, concern for the outsider is a consistent thread running through all the law codes, thus offering a coherent ethical and theological grounding.

The next few paragraphs may be a bit technical, but the details can be illuminating. These brief word studies are suggestive because there seems to be some overlap or imprecision in the usage of these terms. Reasonable generalizations, however, can be gleaned from this summary.

Nokrî/ben-nēkār and zār. These terms often convey that something or someone is non-Israelite.[14] Sometimes this is in a neutral manner. For example, Solomon uses this term to refer to those from other countries who would come to pray to the Lord at the temple in Jerusalem and know the God of Israel (1 Kings 8:41–43). There are occasions, though, where the notion of foreignness in these words has a negative connotation. These terms are used to refer to enemies, strange gods, a licentious woman, or foreign women of another faith who could corrupt an Israelite.[15] In these cases, what is foreign is perceived as bad or threatening.

The term *nokrî* (and sometimes *zār*)[16] can refer to foreigners who dwell in Israel. The profile of the *nokrî* is not altogether clear. The textual evidence that we have suggests at least two nuances. First, there is the impression that at least some of these people have not been in the land very long. David calls his commander Ittai, a Gittite, a *nokrî*. David then says, "You came only yesterday" (2 Sam. 15:19–20). Of course, this phrase is hyperbole, but it implies that Ittai had arrived recently. This might partly explain Ruth's comment to Boaz that she is a *nokriyyâ* (the feminine form of *nokrî*); she had not been in Bethlehem very long and probably felt very out of place.

In other instances, however, it appears that these outsiders did not integrate themselves fully into Israelite life. The law prohibits the *nokrî* from becoming king (Deut. 17:15) and the *ben-nēkār* from participating in some of Israel's rituals (Exod. 12:43; Ezek. 44:7, 9; cf. Lev. 22:25). The *ben-nēkār* could be viewed with suspicion (Ps. 144:7–11). It has been proposed that these individuals may have been foreign merchants or traders who would have had no reason to commit to the community. It seems that an aspect of their "strangeness" within Israel is that these outsiders may have maintained their own faith and customs (Isa. 2:6, yet 1 Kings 8:41, 43). In Israel, where religion was foundational for every dimension of life, refusal to believe in and follow the Lord would have been frowned upon.

Tôšab. The term *tôšab* is even more difficult to define. It occurs only a few times and almost always is found in parallel with either the "hired worker" (Exod. 12:45; Lev. 22:10; 25:6, 40) or "foreigner" (*gēr*; Lev. 25:35, 47; Num. 35:15).[17] That these persons can be hired hands and that they are listed with the sojourner suggests a couple of things. First, these foreigners (or at least some of them) may have been economically dependent. There were reasons for this, and we will return to that socioeconomic reality below. Second, there must have been some distinction between a *tôšab* and a *gēr* for them to be mentioned together. The *tôšab* appears with the *nokrî* in the prohibition about the Passover (Exod. 12:43, 45), so maybe they, too, were not as fully assimilated as the *gēr*. We cannot be certain. The scarcity of verses does not allow for any firm conclusions about these individuals.

Gēr. The most pertinent term for this study is *gēr* (plural, *gērîm*). It occurs over ninety times in the Old Testament. The verbal root (*gûr* I) appears eighty-one times and is usually translated as "sojourn" or "live"; it means to reside in a place not one's own. The noun *gēr* is most prevalent in the legal material of the Pentateuch. Although we are not told where the *gēr* come from, most often they are people of foreign origin (perhaps on occasion internally displaced persons).[18] Either way, these persons are from outside the community. The characteristic that distinguishes the *gēr* from the other categories of outsiders is that the *gēr* has come to settle among God's people. The next section will explore what the books have to say about them. In the English versions, this word has been translated in multiple ways, as "alien," "resident alien," "sojourner," "stranger," "foreigner," and "immigrant."[19]

At least one significant conclusion can be drawn from what has been said thus far. On the basis of their experience and revelation from God, Israel had formulated distinctions between foreigners and made value judgments about them in terms of their integration into the community and their impact on society. The variety in the terminology reflects this. The picture offered by word studies, however, is not altogether clear, so tidy definitions are not possible. At the same time, there is never the negative reaction to the *gēr* that one encounters with the *nokrî* and *zār*.[20]

We probably cannot say much more than that distinctions were made based on Israel's interaction with these foreigners. But this is an important point. It is a natural consequence of having others live among a people. Differences are there for all to see. What will prove to be impressive is to see how God calls his people to respond to the *gēr*.

Laws Pertaining to the Sojourner

Ancient Near Eastern law. The first thing that stands out in the study of the sojourner (*gēr*) in Old Testament law is the remarkable contrast that can be drawn with the other law codes of the ancient Near East. The last chapter mentioned that there is good evidence from administrative documents and other ancient sources about the presence of deportees and other foreign individuals and groups in Assyria, Babylon, and Persia. Nevertheless, the law codes are almost totally silent about these people. There are a few laws that deal with the marital and property rights of someone who leaves for a time and returns (Laws of Eshnunna, §30; Laws of Hammurabi, §§30, 31, 136). Law 41 of the Laws of Eshnunna refers to a foreigner who seems to be a merchant of some kind, but its interpretation is disputed. There were also stipulations in treaties and in correspondence between kingdoms regarding possible obligations to return runaway slaves, free workers, or political refugees.[21]

The legislation in the Old Testament could not be more different. Other ancient law codes reference vulnerable individuals, such as the poor, widows, and orphans, but they are silent about the foreigner. As the chosen people, Israel must figure out what to do with those who come from elsewhere. We find that the laws regarding outsiders are numerous and gracious. What also is extraordinary for that ancient context is that Israel's God is committed to them. As we will see below, the Lord loves them and threatens his people if they mistreat them. In other words, Israel had a theological stake in the presence of the outsiders among them. The obvious question is why? And, what exactly was it?

Life as a sojourner. The economy of Israel was largely agrarian. In the austere environment of that part of the world, life in rural areas could be difficult. In this context, sojourners—those immigrants or refugees who had moved to Israel (or maybe were internally displaced for any variety of reasons)—were a particularly vulnerable group for two principal reasons. On the one hand, the support of kinship groups was indispensable in times of drought, crop failure, disease, and death. The challenge that sojourners faced when arriving in the land was that they had left behind their kinship network. As a result, they were without the help that only an extended family could offer. Sojourners, therefore, could be particularly susceptible to the unexpected and sometimes harsh vicissitudes of life. On the other hand, ownership of land was fundamental for making a living and supporting a family in that peasant economy. Inheritance of property went along kinship lines within Israel, passing from the father to the appropriate male heir (Num. 27:1–11; 36:12; cf. 1 Kings 21:1–3). As foreigners, they were excluded from the land-tenure system.

Without kin and land, many sojourners would be dependent on the Israelites for work, provision, and protection. The fact that the sojourner sometimes is said to be "at the gate" (probably of a town or group of households comprising a village) and is mentioned along with servants and household animals (Exod. 20:10; Deut. 5:14) could suggest that some were day laborers (Deut. 24:14); the Old Testament mentions that some were conscripted to do the hard labor in building the temple (1 Chron. 22:2; 2 Chron. 2:17–18). Apparently a few foreigners did achieve success, but these seem to have been the exception to the rule (Lev. 25:47). Foreigners could be taken advantage of through unfair labor practices, but the law recognized this danger. Sojourners deserved the Sabbath rest from their work like everyone else (Exod. 20:10; Deut. 5:14; cf. Lev. 16:29). They also were to receive their wages in a timely manner (Exod. 23:12; Deut. 24:15), something so important for a group without natural built-in connections and cultural safety nets!

The law recognizes their potentially precarious economic situation and responds by including foreigners with other sectors of the population who would have been at risk too—widows, orphans, and the poor—whom Nicholas Wolterstorff calls the "quartet of the vulnerable."[22] It is not surprising, then, that in defense of his uprightness, Job mentions his hospitality to the *gēr*, along with generosity to those other needy groups (31:32; cf. 29:11–17; 31:13–22, 29–32). Where could the disadvantaged find sustenance? Like other unfortunates, sojourners qualified for the gleaning law. This stipulated that harvesters should leave the edges of a field untouched so that the needy could gather food (Lev. 19:10; 23:22; Deut. 24:19–22). Thus while Ruth is gleaning behind the harvesters, Boaz spots her (Ruth 2). Sojourners also were to receive a portion of the special tithe that was collected every three years for the poor (Deut. 14:28–29; 26:12–13).

Another natural fear of an outsider would be doubts about fair treatment in legal cases. Uncertainties could revolve around, for instance, inadequate language skills, lack of knowledge of the law and customs, and the possibility of prejudice by local folk in judgments. In response, the law stipulates that sojourners are to receive equitable justice. No predisposition against the foreigner was to be tolerated (Deut. 1:16–17) nor any advantage taken because they were powerless (24:17–18; 27:19). Like the native born, sojourners also had access to the cities of refuge (Num. 35:15; Josh. 20:9).

The prophets thundered against those Israelites who did not accept the responsibility to care for these people. It was a breach of their faith in the Lord, and he would not tolerate such disobedience (Jer. 22:3; Ezek. 22:7, 29; Mal. 3:5; cf. Ps. 94:6). Among the proofs of acceptable religion was an ethic of charity toward the disadvantaged, including the sojourner (Jer. 7:4–11; Zech. 7:8–14).

Motivations behind laws. What prompted these laws and elicited those prophetic tirades? What motivations did the Israelites have to provide for these outsiders? At least three are outlined in the biblical text.

First, Israel was to be gracious to the outsider because of their history. Life as sojourners had characterized the experience of the patriarchs and their families (Gen. 23:4; Deut. 26:5; the verb *gwr*, Gen. 12:10; 20:1; 21:23, 34; 26:3; etc.). Israel also had been sojourners many years in Egypt. Unfortunately, that long period as an immigrant people had degenerated into a terrible time of oppression. That bitter experience was to serve as a warning not to mistreat the sojourners in their midst in like manner (Exod. 22:21 [22:20 MT]; 23:9). In fact, God called his people sojourners and hired hands in the land (Lev. 25:23). The land ultimately belonged to God, and the Israelites were there only by his grace. The Lord was the owner and patron of that territory, and Israel's task was to work it in obedience to his laws. They indeed were his day laborers, and that truth was supposed to shape how they dealt with sojourners. What is more, sojourning was a metaphor for living in dependence on the Lord and in his presence, particularly in times of difficulty (e.g., Pss. 5:4 [5:5 MT]; 39:12 [39:13 MT]; 61:4 [61:5 MT]; 119:19; 1 Chron. 29:15).

The command to remember is central to the theology of the book of Deuteronomy and its goal of nurturing Israel's identity as the people of God.[23] Memory is integral to the commands to treat the sojourner well. Israel was to remember that they had sojourned in a foreign land, Egypt (Deut. 10:19 and 23:7 perhaps refer to their days under Joseph), and that they had suffered as slaves there (5:15; 15:15; 16:12; 24:18, 22; cf. 26:6–9). The urging of the people to remember is underscored by the warning not to forget God's works on their behalf (e.g., 4:9, 23; 6:12; 8:11, 14, 19; 26:13; 32:18). Toward these ends, the book puts into place several mechanisms for these stories to be rehearsed periodically in the home, in their communities, and as a nation: the recounting of the historical narrative at the feasts, the annual making of booths, the Sabbath and Passover lessons, and the rehearsing of Moses's song (6:6–9, 20–24; 8:1–20; 16:1–17; 32:1–43). These programmed auditory ("Listen!"), visual ("eyes"), and dramatic (pilgrimage, building booths) performances were designed to re-create those memorable encounters with God for every subsequent generation and to continually engender a decision for God and his ways "today" (this word occurs over sixty times in Deuteronomy), which signifies every day. By remembering and living in accordance with those memories, Israelites affirmed their identity as the people of God. Significantly, this call was inseparable from charitable hospitality toward the vulnerable, including the stranger. The people are reminded that they are the chosen of God and that the land is a gift, but these truths are constantly related to their relationship with those from outside. This unique history of Israel explains why God declares to Israel through Moses, "You shall not oppress the sojourner. *You know the heart of the sojourner,* for you were sojourners in Egypt" (Exod. 23:9, emphasis added). Sojourning was central to their national story.

Second, the charge "Love your neighbor as yourself" (Lev. 19:18), which Jesus called the second greatest commandment (Matt. 22:34–40), was extended to the sojourner precisely because of that experience under Pharaoh: "The foreigner residing among you must be treated as your native-born. Love them as yourself, for you were foreigners in Egypt. I am the LORD your God" (Lev. 19:34). The neighbor to be loved should not be restricted to family or clan members and other native Israelites. The command points to persons beyond those circles, those more difficult to love because of difference. God expected Israelites to nurture a proper and edifying mind-set and to take positive actions toward the immigrant.

Third, the most profound incentive to care for sojourners is to be found in the person of God. In reminding Israel of its history and the obligations that stemmed from it, the Lord explains that the redemption from their experience as foreigners in Egypt also revealed something very important about his person: God loves the helpless, among whom he lists the sojourner (Deut. 10:17–18). This divine love is concrete: God provides food and clothing for the sojourner. Israel is to love sojourners because God does so (Deut. 10:19; cf. Ps. 146:6–9). There can be no stronger argument to support caring for the foreigner! The people of Israel would be the means by which that food and clothing would reach the sojourner; they were to be God's hands and feet. Consequently, to ignore this call of God and the cry of the sojourner is a sin (Deut. 24:14–15). On the other hand, graciousness toward the outsider would be rewarded by divine blessing (Deut. 14:29; 16:15; 24:19; 26:13–15). This kind of divine concern was unheard of in the ancient world.

Ancient Israel did not have government programs and social systems in place as we have today to provide assistance through local, state, and federal channels. Help for the needy had to occur at several levels and through other means: individual families (giving rest on the Sabbath, including sojourners in celebrations), the community (gleaning laws), workplaces (payment of wages, periodic rest), religious centers (collecting of the tithe), and at the city gate with the elders or other legal gatherings (fairness in legal matters). In a sense, *everyone* was involved somehow in the care of the sojourner. The prophets clearly declare that God holds all the people responsible, from individuals to the whole society.

Integration of the sojourner. In the law, we see that Israel opened the most central—and precious—sphere of its life to sojourners: its religion. This faith was foundational to its identity as a people and marked Israel as unique among the nations. Their religious life defined the rhythms of daily, weekly, monthly, and annual life and shaped every aspect of their existence. The sojourner was invited into this world. They were permitted to participate in the Sabbath (Exod. 20:10; Deut. 5:14), the Day of Atonement (Lev. 16:29–30), the Passover (the males would need to be circumcised; Exod. 12:48–49; Num. 9:14), the Feast of Weeks (Deut. 16:11), the Feast of Tabernacles (Deut. 16:14), and the Feast of Firstfruits (Deut. 26:11). Forgiveness for unintentional sin was extended to them (Num. 15:27–29). Tellingly, the sojourner is listed with the rest of the people in the covenant-renewal ceremony of Deuteronomy 29 (vv. 9–15; cf. Josh. 8:33–35).[24]

Expectations and responsibilities most probably would have been placed on sojourners as well. They were to be present at the periodic reading of the law (Deut. 31:10–13; cf. 29:9–15). This makes sense. It would be in listening to the law that sojourners could learn more about what it meant to be a member of that society. Their presence in these gatherings implies that the process of integration had already begun. Listening together with the rest of the people at the Feast of Tabernacles would be a public demonstration of solidarity with Israel and, in turn, of Israel's acceptance of them. This scene also assumes that sojourners spoke and understood Hebrew so that they could follow the reading. Knowing the language would be a prerequisite to participating in the other religious and civic activities too.

Sojourners were to be subject to the penalties of criminal laws (Lev. 24:22), many of the dietary restrictions (Exod. 12:19; Lev. 17:10–15), the sexual taboos (Lev. 18:26), purity laws (Num. 19:10), the regulations for the feasts (Num. 9:14; 15:15), and the prohibition against the worship of other gods and blasphemy against the Lord (Lev. 20:1–2; 24:10–16; Num. 15:30–31). A number of these regulations and several of those cited earlier contain the words "whether he is a native-born Israelite or a foreigner." This expresses in yet another way their equal standing in the community.[25] In the worldview of ancient Israel, the sojourner must not pollute the land by violating these laws; such conduct would result in judgment upon the community (Lev. 17:8–9; 18:24–30).

Still, some distinctions were made between the native-born Israelite and the sojourner. There were dietary laws that did not apply to sojourners (Deut. 14:21), as well as other ritualistic regulations. There was also reluctance to be charitable to certain foreigners and to allow them to participate in civic gatherings (Deut. 23:3–8 [23:4–9 MT]),[26] but there were occasions when this rule was ignored or superseded. Ruth the Moabite is the stellar example of this, and Solomon's prayer of dedication counters it as well (1 Kings 8:41–43).

From the very beginning, Israel had a long history of having persons of other ethnicities in their midst.[27] Not all these relationships were pleasant or beneficial to Israel. We mention several examples, although none are called a *gēr*. Hagar, for example, was an Egyptian in Abraham's household who was forced to flee because of her rift with Sarah, yet Hagar would be promised special care from God (Gen. 16; 21). Israel left Egypt as a "mixed multitude" (Exod. 12:38, 48–49 ESV), and Moses took a Cushite as a wife (Num. 12:1).

Several foreigners rose to prominence in the history of the people. In the book of Joshua, Hagar the Canaanite and Caleb the Kenizzite stand out as key figures. Doeg the Edomite was Saul's chief herdsman (1 Sam. 21:7 [21:8 MT]). Uriah the Hittite was one of David's "mighty men" who came from other lands (2 Sam. 23:37–39). His name (*'ûriyyâ*: "Ya [i.e., Yahweh] is my light") suggests that he was a follower of the God of Israel: his position required absolute loyalty to his king, who tragically would betray him and orchestrate his death in battle (2 Sam. 11). Ittai the Gittite was one of David's commanders who supported David during Absalom's coup (2 Sam. 15:18–22). Phinehas was a Cushite (Exod. 6:16–25; Num. 25; Ps. 106:30–31). The Cushite Ebed-Melek, who befriended Jeremiah during the Babylonian siege, apparently was a mercenary military commander of a Cushite contingent in Jerusalem (Jer. 38–39). The prophet Zephaniah's father was Cushi, possibly suggesting Cushite descent (Zeph. 1:1). In addition to these individuals, the Gibeonites were enfolded into the community as well (Josh. 9; cf. Neh. 3:7–8).

On the negative side of the ledger stand, for instance, the foreign wives of Solomon (1 Kings 3:1; 11:3–8), who helped lead the king away from true faith in Yahweh, and Ahab's wife Jezebel, a princess from Phoenician Sidon (1 Kings 16–19; 2 Kings 9:30–37). They reflect arranged marriages—a common practice at the time—between kingdoms for political, economic, and military reasons. These women entered with no apparent regard for the faith of Israel, unlike the *gērîm*, who had come to Israel in need and to become constructive members of national life.

Ruth. The most expansive description of a foreigner's integration into Israel is presented in the book of Ruth. The account is located during the period of the judges in a time of famine. In order to survive, Elimelek, his wife Naomi, and their sons Mahlon and Kilion leave Bethlehem in Judah. They cross the Jordan and migrate to the plains of Moab. There the sons marry Moabite women, Orpah and Ruth (1:1–2). Said another way, these two daughters-in-law of Naomi marry immigrants

(Naomi's two sons). Within a span of just a few verses, the narrative provides a second instance of migration—in the opposite direction. Elimelek dies soon after the family's arrival in Moab, and within ten years the two sons die as well (1:3–5). The three widows now are left to provide for themselves. Naomi hears that the Lord is providing food for his people back in Bethlehem and decides to return to her people and hometown (1:6–7). She tries to convince her daughters-in-law to go back to their families, and eventually Orpah remains in Moab (1:8–14). Ruth, however, decides to accompany Naomi on her journey to reestablish herself in Bethlehem.

These two solitary women—one an Israelite, the other a foreign dependent related by marriage—arrive in the town, but they struggle to make ends meet. Their situations are now reversed: Naomi the immigrant has come home; Ruth, who had married an immigrant, becomes an immigrant in a strange land. Ironically, the challenge continues to be having enough to eat. The younger woman goes to the fields to gather food to support her Israelite mother-in-law and herself. Eventually her hard work as a gleaner and her stellar character incur the favor of Naomi's kinsman, Boaz. He redeems Naomi's property and marries Ruth. Through Boaz's marriage to this Moabite and the son born of that relationship, the ancestral piece of land can remain within the family. Boaz fulfills his familial obligation to Naomi, but he does not do this grudgingly. Boaz is generous to Ruth, an immigrant woman in need, and extends protection and provision to her and Naomi through marriage. What makes Boaz's actions even more noteworthy is that Ruth is a Moabite, a people that Israel's traditions (Num. 22–25; cf. Ezra 9:1–2) and law (Deut. 23:3; cf. Neh. 13:1–3, 23) did not view favorably.[28]

The book of Ruth can be read in several rich ways. Studies on the legal background concerning the gleaning, property, and inheritance shed light on the account's details. It can be appreciated, too, as an exemplary lesson in mercy and faithfulness, both between individuals and as sovereign blessings from God.[29]

For our purposes, the book also can be read as an immigrant story.[30] Assimilation theory can be helpful here.[31] This approach looks at how immigrants acquire the requisite sociocultural competencies to move into their new context. It proposes that there are three kinds of mechanisms immigrants need to succeed in the new setting: *purposive action, networks and forms of human capital,* and *institutional avenues.*

As to the first component of assimilation, Ruth takes the initiative by famously declaring her commitment to Naomi as they set out (1:14–18). There is an interesting dynamic at this point in the narrative. Why does Ruth decide not to go back to her Moabite family as Orpah does? Would her status as a childless widow of a foreigner have carried a stigma? One also wonders why Naomi says nothing when Ruth states that she will leave all and cling to her. There is no acknowledgment, no expression of gratitude for this selfless resolution. Is part of Naomi's bitterness (1:15, 20–21) directed at Moab, the land where her husband and sons died? How does she evaluate what Ruth is doing? Is her silence designed to discourage Ruth, or is it a sign of her resignation to her misfortunes? She is returning empty-handed, surely not what she had hoped for. The reader can only speculate. Other purposive actions taken by Ruth include her initiative to glean, her interaction with Boaz in chapter 2, and her actions at the threshing floor in chapter 3, which could have backfired horribly and left her with a bad reputation.

Engaging the networks in Bethlehem, the second component in the assimilation process, brings another set of challenges for Ruth. She needs to interact with and gain the acceptance of the town's women, the reapers, and the elders, even as she navigates the foreign environment of her new dwelling with her mother-in-law. Things do not seem to begin well. When Ruth and Naomi arrive in Bethlehem, she is not introduced to the townsfolk. Ruth is not mentioned in the scene. Has Naomi ignored her? Is she embarrassed by the presence of a Moabite daughter-in-law? Perhaps the people do not engage

Ruth because they are suspicious of her ethnicity. Is there awkwardness in that scene? Does Ruth stand silent, uncomfortably off to the side, as the women engage Naomi? In chapter 2 the workers single her out as a Moabite (by her clothing? an accent?), although they notice her work ethic (2:6–7). Ruth calls herself a "foreign woman" (*nokriyyâ*; 2:10) and a "servant" (2:13). Does she feel out of place and marginalized? No one knows her name; perhaps no one had even asked. She is simply an outsider, the woman who returned with Naomi.

Boaz is immediately supportive. He values Ruth's efforts on behalf of her mother-in-law, as well as the sacrifice she has made to leave her original family, land, and culture to come to Judah, and says a blessing over her (2:11–12). Boaz also recognizes her vulnerability as a single woman among the men, something that concerns Naomi too (2:15, 22). He shares food with her and allows her to gather freely. In chapter 3 he accepts his role as kinsman-redeemer and sends her on her way with more food. By the end of chapter 4, Ruth is married and has won the respect of the elders in the town. They compare her with Rachel and Leah (who also were from outside the land). This Moabite immigrant reverses any negative stereotypes of her people that the townspeople may have had and is compared to two women who played significant roles in Israel's history (4:11–12)! The women, who had not noticed (or maybe ignored) Ruth at her arrival, praise God for the child and commend Ruth's love of Naomi (4:14–15).

What of Naomi? Naomi is still silent and does not respond to the women's words. But she does embrace Ruth's son, Obed. The one who had bemoaned that she had come back empty (1:20–21) now has someone to care for her in her old age, and she will be his nurse (4:15–17). Surely this boy from a bicultural marriage would not experience what his immigrant mother had, nor would he need to struggle, as she had done, to gain entry into the life of that community. It would be home for him from the start. Bethlehem, too, would be a different place after its inclusion of this Moabite woman and her son, probably with a new appreciation of the people who lived on the other side of the Dead Sea.

The third component of assimilation theory deals with the institutional avenues. In the case of Ruth, these are the pertinent laws mentioned above, laws related to gleaning, inheritance, the redemption of property, and perhaps levirate marriage. Her actions in the story suggest that she is aware of these and applies them to her situation.

Is Ruth able to integrate herself into Bethlehem? Does she find full acceptance? What does she retain of her Moabite background and for how long? We will never know. The reader can sense that ethnic boundaries do not totally disappear. The townspeople never call Ruth by name. To the reapers she is simply the "Moabite" (2:6); to those at the gate she is "the woman" (4:11) and "this young woman" (4:12); to the women of the town, "your daughter-in-law" (4:15). Even Boaz in public refers to her as "Ruth the Moabite" (4:5, 10). To the narrator, though, she can simply be "Ruth" (2:8; 4:13).

Whatever her personal level of integration into that Judean town, the genealogy of the final verses of the book reveals that her story is connected to the lineage of David (4:17b–22). In her wildest imaginings, could she ever have dreamed that her experiences were part of something so significant? In the New Testament she appears in the genealogy of Jesus (Matt. 1:5)! What is more, every year Jews read the book of Ruth for the Feast of Weeks (Shavuot) and commemorate this foreign peasant woman who became part of the community of Bethlehem in Judah. This life—the exemplary striving and hardships of a widowed immigrant—was a key element in the plan of God.

Future hope. Finally, there is the prophetic hope that one day the connection between sojourner and native Israelite would be closer. Ezekiel 47:21–23 envisions a time when sojourners will inherit land along with the tribes of Israel. The barrier against possessing their own parcels of the promised land will be done away with. When Isaiah talks of the future ingathering of Israel from exile and depicts their coming to worship at Zion, the holy mountain of God, he includes the "foreigner" (56:1–8; cf. 2:2–4; 14:1). Interestingly, he uses the term *ben-nēkār*, not *gēr*.[32] These are people from other lands who will seek to love the Lord, echoing that hope of Solomon in 1 Kings 8:41–43. Foreigner and Israelite together will enjoy his presence in glorious fashion. The breadth of God's mercy and the response of the peoples of the world to his person will not be limited to native-born persons or to the boundaries of Israel.

We began this section by declaring that Israel's law was unique in its treatment of the outsider, both in the number of laws and in their generosity. This is unlike some who have argued that these laws distinguish between "legal" and "illegal" immigrants.[33] Nothing in the laws suggests this distinction that dominates current debates. Could there have been some sort of legal means to secure entry and residency in ancient Israel? Perhaps, but nothing along this vein appears anywhere in the biblical text. Was there a formal monitoring of the flow of persons across Israel's borders? Again, maybe, but nothing of the sort is mentioned. Instead, the text presents a surprising openness for the ancient world.

This review of immigration laws and customs, especially regarding their motivations, provides an answer to the question of why Israel's laws are different from the law codes of the surrounding peoples. It is because of Israel's special story and the character of the Lord that they were commanded to treat the sojourner in such a caring manner. Their concern for the vulnerable from another land was fundamental to their witness and life as the people of God.

Implications for Today

Different concepts of law. This cursory survey of Old Testament legislation dealing with the sojourner can be instructive in several ways. First of all, the short discussion on law and culture that is informed by cultural anthropology is pertinent.

Because foreigners come from another culture, their concept of law will differ from the way it is understood in this country.

For example, my life has been spent straddling North American and Latin American cultures. One major difference between the two, to which anyone who has traveled or lived south of the border can attest, is the different appreciation for the meaning and practice of law. This can easily be empirically verified by anyone at a personal level, for instance, by trying to obtain a driver's license, get a visa, pay a fine, conduct a bank transaction, or get a package from a customs house. It quickly becomes apparent that law and laws are inseparable from bureaucratic protocol and artificial (but very important!) cultural formalities, social status, and family connections.

These attitudes and the nature of laws can be traced to a cultural history quite distinct from that of the United States. Latin American law has its origins on the Iberian Peninsula, not in a British heritage. Their different branches of government also identify their functions and rights in ways that are different from this country. These and other factors yield a very dissimilar legal culture, which impacts politics and the world of business and their corresponding legal values and structures. In Latin America, all of this is normal and natural; it is the way things have always been, and change comes slowly. Latin America would not be Latin America without this inherited spice of life. The majority culture in the United States should anticipate that immigrants' adaptation to the laws and legal ethos of the host country will take time. Latin American immigrants (and those from elsewhere) will need to listen to and acquaint themselves with the law of the land (cf. Deut. 31:10–13).

Varied experiences. Second, the Old Testament presents a realistic picture of an ancient society trying to come to grips with a complex social reality. Several terms are applied to outsiders. Even though it is hard to make definitive comments about their meanings, the fact that there are multiple labels for foreigners in Israel suggests that the experiences with outsiders were varied and that these individuals could be evaluated in different ways. Today this pattern is also true of the majority culture's appraisal of "Others," people who have come from elsewhere. In other words, a variety of reactions to the arrival and presence of immigrants, today's sojourners, is to be expected.

Law as paradigm. A third point is based on Christopher Wright's thesis that the law of Israel is a paradigm for other nations. It was to be a tangible illustration of the ethical orientation for life that God intended for all humanity. The next component of this model (not developed earlier in this book) is Wright's contention that the moral values of Israel's law, which found expression in specific regulations for that ancient context, also are pertinent to the modern era. That is, Deuteronomy 4:5–8 points beyond its specific time and setting. The law that God gave through Moses was intended to be an object lesson to the surrounding nations then *and even now*. The structures, institutions, and other initiatives corresponding to those same values will obviously look different today than they did millennia ago. But God's enduring ethical ideals are still valid and should be systemically made concrete in the contemporary world.

Care for the sojourner is one of those ideals. It was a moral demand that set God's people apart from the other nations; even more significantly, it was grounded in God's very person. Not to be hospitable, individually or collectively, merited condemnation by the prophets. The law reflects an awareness that sojourners are vulnerable, and it offers a series of mechanisms to meet their needs. To this charitable socioeconomic and legal framework is added an invitation to the sojourner into what was making Israel into the Israel that God desired: its religious life.

If what Wright proposes is correct, and I believe it is, then the imperative of caring for the sojourner is binding on every nation. At the very least, this ethical commitment should resonate especially with the people of God in the majority culture and in their churches. It ought to be demonstrated in specific measures that respond to the needs of immigrants. The means will vary according to the opportunities and limitations in any given context, but the responsibility remains. In addition, if this moral imperative is for all nations, then these Christians have the obligation to be a voice for God's heart, caring for the sojourner in the broader society and in the country at large.

The Bible does not provide a blueprint for action or modern legislation, but it does clarify the spiritual and moral call. Some criticize the statements on immigration by various Christian denominations and organizations as underinformed about (or willfully ignoring) the workings of national polity, such as matters pertaining to citizenship and the strictures of the international community of nation-states. These statements are said to be too vague and overly moralistic in their analysis to offer a substantive contribution to the national debate.[34] This is a valid concern (which would need to be established on a case-by-case basis). From the perspective of this chapter, the purpose of looking at biblical laws is to ascertain a *moral compass* for Christians as they enter these discussions or try to take part in the sociopolitical arena. The proper role of God's law is to point us in an ethical direction and provide moral criteria.

Historical memory. In addition to the varied responses and the moral imperative, there is yet another lesson to be learned. Care for the sojourner was important for Israel because they, too, had experienced life as sojourners—sometimes in most unpleasant ways. At their feasts they rehearsed Israel's history as immigrants in Egypt; these reminders to be gracious to outsiders were exercises in collective memory. All of this was crucial for their formation as a people of virtue, especially the virtue of generous hospitality. Stated another way, the arrival and presence of sojourners were *not a threat to Israel's national identity*; rather, their presence was *fundamental to the very meaning of their identity*. The people of Israel could not be who they were supposed to be before God and the world if they forgot who they had been and from where they had come. In addition, concern for sojourners was part of an expansive ethical vision for the needy that included widows, orphans, and the poor. Believers cannot divorce vulnerable groups with whom they do not want to relate from the comprehensive biblical call to incarnate God's presence and care for all in need.

While the text is speaking about ancient Israel, there may be analogies with the United States. Today some deny that this country should be understood as a nation of immigrants. It is said that there have always been restrictions and preferential quotas and that the country has been ambivalent toward those from other lands. This is true, but what this position cannot deny is that for two and a half centuries there has been a constant flow of immigrants—with or without quotas, by stipulated processes or without proper documents—arriving at the nation's borders. The numbers vary, the color of the faces may change, but the reality of continual immigration is an indisputable fact. Immigration is inseparable from the history of the nation and is fundamental to its identity.

Every family can point back to parents, grandparents, or great-grandparents who came from somewhere else. It is part of our familial memory, but at the national level we have collective amnesia. What we celebrate are pale vestiges of immigrant memories that are often reduced to a parade and food and drink (St. Patrick's Day, Oktoberfest, Columbus Day, Cinco de Mayo). What has been forgotten are the prejudices and the marginalization of those earlier immigrants, the ghettoes, and the exploitation of their labor. To deny the hard and unpleasant parts of the past in order to sanitize the present and shape the future as we would like it to be might be a greater threat to national identity in the United States. Such a threat is why the law exhorts Israel to remember their *slavery* in Egypt, not to forget that cauldron of exploitation.

Laws, especially as they pertain to the vulnerable (widows, orphans, the poor, outsiders, and other groups), can be a window into a country's soul. What do these laws reveal about us and the breadth and depth of our compassion? Ideally, measures designed to appropriately deal with immigration and immigrants should reflect the virtues of kindness, generosity, and patience instead of being motivated by fear or prejudice. To be sure, public policy and legislation must be pragmatically realistic in terms of administrative controls, economic need and impact, educational initiatives, law enforcement, and the like. The key is to explore options and to ground these measures in divine compassion and wisdom, not in a punitive, exclusionary spirit. All these reflections underscore that migration matters are inescapably systemic.

Broad responsibility. As mentioned previously, we observe that the responsibility to take care of the sojourner in Israel was carried out at many levels: through families, religious centers, and other local initiatives. This was necessitated because of the nature of the ancient context. The modern world is different. Still, while today the government is usually expected to handle such matters, there is value in a multipronged approach. Wider participation yields deeper social awareness and ethical concern.

Multiple reactions. There are lessons as well for the immigrant, one of which must be sober realism. The evidence provided by our discussion on the terminology used to refer to foreigners in the Old Testament should lead these sojourners to anticipate diverse reactions to their coming here. Sometimes those who are native-born persons will qualify the term "foreign" in a neutral fashion, simply as a label; on other occasions foreignness will be prejudiced and considered negatively. In the greater number of instances, however, immigrants may experience the welcome of the majority culture. In their labors, they may also benefit from the generosity of individuals of the majority culture and the "safety net" afforded by this country's legislation (such as schooling for children and emergency-room care) and by a myriad of independent organizations and Christian ministries. The United States does not have a law revealed from heaven, and so the legal system is imperfect and is now being contested; it needs to be reformed to better handle current circumstances. Thus there are times when the laws will be helpful, and there are other times when they can be contradictory, frustratingly complicated, unreasonable, and even unjust.

Cultural accommodation. The Old Testament law makes clear that there were expectations for the sojourner, just as there were demands on Israel. Some of the Christian literature that champions the immigrants draws from the law only a few verses that command the care of the sojourner. This can be a strategic decision to convince audiences of the urgency to provide for needy immigrants, with which I wholeheartedly agree. But such an approach can be one-sided and incomplete. Israel's law assumes that there is movement on the part of the sojourner toward the host culture (Israel): learning its ways and its language and respecting its laws and taboos, even coming to believe in its God. Accordingly, there are cases of exemplary foreigners who moved to and lived within Israel.

What we will never know is to what extent these individuals accommodated themselves to the culture of Israel and how much of their home culture they retained; surely it would have differed for each one. For instance, countless Latinos and Latinas are trying to learn the ways of the United States; they appreciate the importance of learning English and want to be respectful of American customs. I have heard this commitment from Hispanic pastors who are counseling their people toward these ends. I have seen it in immigrant families who are trying to better their lives here and raise their children in constructive ways. Adaptation is occurring, but how much of home is retained will depend on a variety of factors relative to each person, family, and community. This scenario becomes more complicated with time, across generations, and with intermarriages between immigrants and native-born individuals. The culture, as it has always done, is absorbing elements of immigrant cultures. From the Latino side, music, food, soccer, films, and much more. The demographics and landscape of the United States are changing, and immigration is at the heart of the new America.

Conclusion

The first chapter on the Old Testament highlighted the theme of all people being in the image of God and then demonstrated some of the many experiences of living in other countries in the biblical text. This chapter began with hospitality and then explored the laws regarding the sojourner. Other issues in the Old Testament could be relevant to the immigration debate, but I end my reflections here.

The goal has been to uncover a biblical point of view—or, perhaps better, a more biblically grounded attitude—toward immigrants and migration. It is a topic close to the heart of God and inseparable from the life and mission of God's people. Openness to outsiders is a virtue, and concern for their well-being is manifested tangibly in Old Testament law. For their part, foreigners were to respond in positive ways to this invitation to enter the world of Israel.

These truths should help orient how Christians of the majority culture *and* immigrant Christians wrestle with the current quandary. With hearts attuned to the will of God, perhaps the tenor of the debate can be leavened with grace and any proposed solutions and compromises can be guided by divine wisdom. The next chapter will complement what has been presented thus far with the contribution of the New Testament.

3

Entertaining Angels Unawares

Hospitality for the Stranger in the New Testament

Up to this point, our attention has been on the Old Testament. What might the New Testament contribute to the biblical material on migration and immigrants and refugees? This chapter begins with the person and teaching of Jesus. But from the outset, this starting point can be challenging—and frustrating. The reason is that today Jesus comes in many shapes and colors. One has only to enter "images of Jesus" in Google's search engine and click. Instantly, hundreds of different portrayals of Jesus are available. He appears as Caucasian, African American, Caribbean, Asian, black African, and some sort of Hispanic. Jesus can be meek or manly, pious or warlike, an Eastern Orthodox mystic or a Che Guevara look-alike, a beggar or an entrepreneur who gives guidance to CEOs. The possibilities are as varied as the human imagination. Jesus takes on the form of the beholder, amenable to that person's view of life.

This tendency also holds true in academic circles. Numerous publications argue that the historical Jesus was not the divine Son of God of Christian orthodoxy but instead, for instance, a peasant cynic or a mystic. The appeal of *The Da Vinci Code* and the claims associated with the Gospel of Judas and other apocryphal gospels testify not only to the power that Jesus holds over the general public but also to the fascination that people have with alternative views that reduce Jesus to the merely human. More circumspect scholarship has been focusing anew on the Jewish background of Jesus and the trustworthiness of the canonical Gospel accounts.[1]

This more confident orientation is helpful as we go to the Gospels for insights into the immigration debate. How so? If one claims to be a follower of Jesus, then what is reported in the Gospels about what Jesus said and did can be trusted and matters. A better sense of the sociocultural context of Jesus's time can also help us better understand the ethical demands he made that still have a claim on Christians.

Interestingly, a reading of the four Gospels reveals that Jesus never dealt directly with the topic of migration. At the same time, however, he did give attention to others who were not Jews, to the marginalized, and to those deemed less valuable as persons (such as women and lepers). If the good news that he announced was for all humankind, then Jesus needed to expand his disciples' vision to embrace all kinds of people. For his followers and others who heard him, cultural identity was a fundamental issue. If the immigration discussion concerns cultural identity—and it clearly does—then it is important for Christians to see how Jesus dealt with those who were different and to learn from his teaching on such things.

This chapter, therefore, begins with a look at material in the Gospels. I will highlight two experiences of Jesus and then discuss his teaching that is pertinent to our topic.[2] The second section turns to the First Epistle of Peter and other passages that utilize the language of sojourner in reference to Christians and the church. The third section returns to the theme of hospitality that we looked at in the previous chapter. The last section briefly examines Romans 13. This passage brings up the question of legality. Undocumented immigrants have violated laws of the United States, and that inescapable fact, it is said, should set the parameters of discussions concerning immigration. I have left discussion of Romans 13 until last for a reason. It is the place to end our survey, not the place to begin the conversation.

Learning from Jesus

Jesus the Refugee

Not long after Jesus was born, he and his parents had to leave Bethlehem. The Gospel of Matthew informs us that Herod the Great wanted to kill him (Matt. 2:13–14). Herod had been told by the magi that they were on their way to see the newborn king of the Jews (2:1–8). History tells us that Herod was fearful of potential rivals to his throne and ruthless with anyone he considered disloyal. He became increasingly cruel and paranoid toward the end of his life (he died in 4 BC), executing even his favorite wife, Mariamne, and several of his sons. When the magi did not report back, Herod ordered the slaughter of all the young boys in the area around Bethlehem (2:16–18). Bethlehem was a village, so the number probably was not large (some estimate about 20), but eliminating innocent children was symptomatic of Herod's mercilessness.[3]

Joseph, Mary, and the child Jesus sought asylum in Egypt, beyond the reach of Herod's jurisdiction. (How many others might have fled there to escape Herod?) A large Jewish population resided in Egypt, especially in Alexandria, so they may have gone there. Bethlehem lay about 80 miles from the Egyptian border, with Alexandria a further 200 miles.[4] The family left in haste after the angel's warning, most likely taking few possessions with them in order to travel quickly and avoid Herod's troops. There are no details of the sojourn in Egypt, and Matthew is the only Gospel that records it. The stay in Egypt was short, anywhere from several months to two years. In time, an angel informed the family that Herod had died (2:19–21). They first had wanted to go to Joseph's ancestral town, Bethlehem, but Herod's son Archelaus now was reigning over Judea. His reputation for cruelty was reminiscent of his father's (2:22), so Joseph instead took the family north to Nazareth in Galilee.

The joy of the nativity scene and the wonder of the visit of the magi are overshadowed by the tragic account of the senseless death of the little boys of Bethlehem and the flight of refugees. The migration of this family locates the Jesus story within a movement that spans history, of people desiring to flee misery and the threat of death.

Jesus and Outsiders

The setting. First-century Palestine was a complicated place.[5] Geographically, it was divided into several regions. On the west side of the Dead Sea, the Jordan River, and the Sea of Galilee, from north to south, were most of Galilee, then Samaria, Judea, and Idumea; across the Jordan were Peraea and the Decapolis. Politics were knotty. The area was under the sovereignty of the Roman Empire, but there was considerable autonomy. Depending on local circumstances and history, the empire appointed regional governors or permitted others, such as Herod, to rule limited kingdoms. In return, Rome expected these proxies to collect taxes, keep the peace, and maintain loyalty to Caesar. Palestine was volatile, with strong political rivalries and a vocal population that was unafraid to appeal to Rome to express their discontent.

The religious world also was complex. The gods of Greco-Roman religion, the mystery cults, and emperor worship had their adherents. Divisions within the Jewish faith added more confusion to the religious landscape. Among the Jews in Judea were several sects, the most significant being the Pharisees, the

Sadducees, and the Essenes. Although the Pharisees were the most influential group in terms of setting the agenda for religious practices, evidently much of the populace did not align itself formally with any of these groups. Under Herod, Jerusalem had become a world-class city, and pilgrims from all around came to worship at its temple and participate in the Jewish festivals (cf. Acts 2:5–11).

The New Testament presents Jesus as moving within and speaking into this context. Jesus engages Jews from a wide spectrum of theological and social positions, and he is in contact with Gentiles from early on in his ministry in several geographical settings (e.g., Matt. 8:5–13; 15:21–28; Mark 3:7–8; 7:31; and parr.). For the purposes of this section, though, the discussion will concentrate on a specific group, the Samaritans.[6]

The Samaritans resided within the region of Samaria. They practiced a form of Judaism but had a different holy mountain (Mount Gerizim), their own priesthood, and distinct beliefs and rituals. They were not accepted as equals by Jews, and there was a deep antipathy between the two populations. Samaritans were despised because to the Jews they represented a perversion of the faith of Abraham, Isaac, and Jacob. Over the centuries the antagonism was marked by a series of betrayals and acts of revenge. In 128 BC the Jewish leader Hyrcanus took over Samaria and burned down the Samaritan sanctuary on Mount Gerizim; in 107 BC he destroyed Shechem. In AD 6/7 some Samaritans infiltrated the Passover celebration in Jerusalem and scattered bones in the temple, thereby defiling it. Other incidents occurred after the time of Jesus and confirm the ongoing animosity. For example, in AD 52 Samaritans killed a company of pilgrims from Galilee who were on their way to Jerusalem for Passover. This atrocity degenerated into a spiral of violence that led to several interventions by the Roman authorities.

This hostility is the backdrop for the ministry of Jesus to Samaritans and his appeal to them in his teaching. For a Jew, doing anything charitable for a Samaritan or saying something favorable about them would elicit scorn from fellow Jews. The disciples' dislike of the Samaritans is illustrated by their reaction to a Samaritan village's rejection of Jesus (Luke 9:51–56). James and John, the "sons of thunder" (Mark 3:17), want to call down fire from heaven, perhaps as Elijah had done so many years before (1 Kings 18; 2 Kings 1). To the Jews, Samaritans were more than religious outsiders; they were also enemies.

Jesus's personal encounters. The best-known story of Jesus engaging Samaritans is found in the Gospel of John, chapter 4: the account of his conversation with the woman at Jacob's well. This chapter is often cited in discussions about cross-cultural missions, which can be a suitable appropriation of the account.[7] Instead, I concentrate more particularly on the significance of Jesus, a rabbi, speaking with a Samaritan—more specifically, a Samaritan woman. Jewish tradition regarded Samaritan women as unclean; they were categorized as menstruants from the cradle.[8] That this woman is of questionable repute (so say some interpreters) would make Jesus's dialogue with her even more impressive (John 4:16–18). The extraordinariness of what he does is recognized by the woman herself: "You are a Jew and I am a Samaritan woman. How can you ask me for a drink?" It is emphasized by the text's side comment: "For Jews do not associate with Samaritans" (4:9).

At this point in the narrative, Jesus is traveling from Judea to Galilee with his disciples. Geographically, Samaria lay between the two. It is commonly said that Jesus chose not to take the circuitous route along the eastern side of the Jordan River, which Jews could follow to avoid ritual contamination and confrontation with Samaritans, so that he could have this encounter. Though the decision to take the longer route may have been made by some Jews, others preferred the shorter, more direct way, even though the trip through Samaria might not be pleasant.

The text says, "Now he *had* to go through Samaria" (4:4, emphasis added). The English "he had" translates a form of the Greek impersonal verb *deō*. A literal rendering of the line could be "Now *it was necessary* for him to go through Samaria" (the same verb appears earlier in 3:7, 14, 30). This is the road required to journey north, but another level of necessity is at work. The occasion is an important part of what Jesus needs to do for his mission. This meeting is not a coincidental happenstance; it is part of Jesus's predetermined plan.

His disciples had gone ahead to buy food, but Jesus sits at the well and waits. The woman arrives alone to draw water. Normally, women would go in groups to do this work. If she has not been chaste, perhaps she would go alone out of shame or because she was shunned by other women. Jesus asks her to serve him water. A Jewish rabbi is speaking to a Samaritan woman and asking her for help! This is remarkable in its countercultural effect. If he were to drink water from a vessel given to him by this woman, Jesus would render himself ritually impure. Jesus, however, does not hesitate. In the give-and-take of their exchange, Jesus leads the woman to consider divine living water (4:10–15) and true worship (4:19–24). At the end Jesus reveals that he is Messiah (4:25–26). Although it is impossible to know what the woman actually understands about Jesus at this point, she runs to bring others to hear him (4:28–30), and many believe (4:39–42). Those who respond are visible evidence that the harvest indeed is at hand (4:34–38), and it is beginning in Samaria—with Samaritans!

Another incident with a Samaritan is found in the Gospel of Luke, chapter 17. Jesus is close to Samaria, verse 11 says, so we do not know if the village he enters was located in Samaria or Galilee. Since Jesus is headed south to Jerusalem, it could very well have been in Samaria. There he hears ten lepers calling out to him (Luke 17:11–13). They stand at a distance because, according to Jewish purity laws, their disease makes them unclean (Lev. 13:45–46; Num. 5:2–3). Jesus tells them to go and present themselves to the priests, as stipulated in the law for those who have been cured (Lev. 13:19; 14:1–11). Miraculously, they are cured on their journey. Only one of the ten, though, returns to thank him with humility and gratitude, throwing himself at Jesus's feet in praise to God.

At this point, the text provides information that it has held back until this moment: "And he was a Samaritan" (Luke 17:16). Once more the faith of a Samaritan is exemplary. This scene is ironic. Jesus is on his way to the Holy City, where he will be rejected by the Jews, but this "foreigner" believes (17:18). It is possible that Jesus's parting words to the man mean that he alone of the ten achieved full reconciliation with God (17:19).[9]

In both encounters, the individuals whom Jesus engages are doubly outcast. Both are Samaritans. What is more, the first may have been morally suspect, and the second is a leper. Jesus transcends the long-standing enmity between the Jews and Samaritans. He accepts the Others, and they accept him. In all of this, Jesus never ceases to be a Jew. Yet he can integrate his cultural core with other transcendent commitments and gracious attitudes that move him beyond the closed society of many of his peers.

Jesus's teaching. The teaching of Jesus, like his actions, is designed in part to push the boundaries of the understanding of his followers. Jesus models a new and different way of looking at persons who are beyond the circle of acceptability. He displays this in his treatment of those who are the marginalized of society (women, the poor, the sick) and those who are outsiders (gentiles and Samaritans). What he teaches reinforces and explains that lived commitment. Two passages are especially relevant. The first also deals with a Samaritan, while the second mentions the "stranger" in the context of the final judgment.

Throughout his ministry Jesus had exchanges with religious leaders. Some had sincere motives and wanted to comprehend God better; others probed Jesus for less noble reasons, trying to trick him into making self-incriminating statements. The latter appears to be the case in the Gospel of Luke, chapter 10. A scribe, "an expert in the law," confronts Jesus with a question about eternal life (Luke 10:25). Jesus responds with another question that challenges the scribe: "What is written in the

Law? . . . How do you read it?" (10:26). The scribe answers by saying that one must follow the command to love God (Deut. 6:5) and neighbor (Lev. 19:18). Jesus agrees and commands that he obey these injunctions (Luke 10:27–28).

Something in Jesus's response spurs the scribe to ask a follow-up question: "And who is my neighbor?" (10:29). He is soliciting a definition as to whom he, as a Jew, should love. Within that context, the scribe may have been wondering if the neighbor should be limited to his own religious circle or perhaps include any member of the Jewish community. Jesus replies with what is now called the parable of the good Samaritan (10:30–37).[10]

In this parable, a priest and a Levite pass by a man who has been attacked by robbers. The scene and the description are very realistic for those days, so the story would have captured the audience's attention. No motive is given for why the religious leaders avoid the injured man, but it can be assumed that they fear contamination by one who may be dead (10:30; cf. Lev. 21:1–3, 10–11; Num. 19:11–19). After they depart from the scene, the audience would have anticipated that the next person in the story would be a lay Jew, who would demonstrate a purer, simpler faith. Instead, surprisingly, that person is a Samaritan! The Samaritan not only stops to treat the wounds of the man but he also takes him to an inn, cares for the man there, and then promises to pay for anything that might be needed in his absence. All of this is done without any expectation of recompense from this victim who has lost everything.

The question that had been posed to Jesus was "Who is my neighbor?" The parable complicates what the scribe expected to hear. Jesus asks, "Which of these three do you think was [literally, "became"] a neighbor to the man who fell into the hands of robbers?" (10:36). Remember that the original issue had been to identify the neighbor whom the scribe should love. The neighbor in the parable is the person who helps the robbed man. This neighbor is a Samaritan, a scorned enemy. *He* is the neighbor whom the scribe is to love! Jesus forces him to acknowledge this truth with his question. The scribe responds correctly, but he cannot bring himself to say "the Samaritan." The benevolent person is simply called "the one who had mercy on him" (10:37). Jesus concludes their exchange by telling the scribe to emulate that neighbor, the Samaritan, in order to fulfill the command to love. Again, the people of God are taught about true faith through one outside of and rejected by their culture.

The second passage is the discourse of Matthew 25:31–46. This is part of the longer exchange between Jesus and the disciples on the Mount of Olives before his arrest, trial, and crucifixion (24:1–25:46). In these well-known verses, Jesus speaks about the final judgment of the nations. This passage draws on imagery from the Old Testament and other Jewish literature.[11] In those texts God usually functions as the judge, but there are cases where judgment is performed by another end-time figure whom God appoints. In Matthew 25 that individual is "the Son of Man," who acts in the name of his Father. The decision regarding merited eternal blessing or judgment is based on how people treat "the least of these brothers and sisters of mine" and thereby also treat the Son of Man, the King on his glorious throne (25:40).

These verses are relevant to the immigration discussion because of the use of the word *stranger* (or *foreigner*, Greek *xenos*)[12] in verses 35, 38, 43, 44. This term is included with the hungry, thirsty, naked, sick, and imprisoned. The lengthy list of the needy in and of itself is not unique to Jesus. Similar concerns are found in many passages in the Old Testament and other ancient documents.[13] Some believe that the list underscores the breadth of Jesus's compassion, as well as the divine ethical demand placed on all humanity. What is particularly impactful is that *Jesus identifies himself* with each vulnerable type of person: "I was . . ."

But who are the "least of these"? There are several interpretive options. Some make the case that the reference is broad, that it refers to any vulnerable person. To ignore any of these "little ones," it is argued, is tantamount to refusing Jesus him-self.[14] Since the "stranger" is included, we have here the moral imperative to take care of the immigrant or refugee. In addition, if this passage is placed against the wider framework of the image of God, to neglect any vulnerable person is essentially to turn away from God as well.

Many interpreters, however, go in a different direction. In the Gospel of Matthew, "little ones" refers to the disciples of Jesus (10:42; 18:6, 10, 14), as do his "brothers and sisters" (except when the reference is to earthly siblings).[15] This passage, therefore, could speak of the hardships that Christians in general will suffer from agents of the nations[16] or, more specifically, what the messengers of the gospel will endure.[17] The theme of the opposition they will face as they go out in Jesus's name appears earlier, when he sends out the Twelve (10:11–42). According to this view, to scorn the disciples and their message is to reject Jesus, the one who is the essence of that message and who commissions the disciples. Their future itinerant ministry would make them "strangers" wherever they go. Accordingly, within the trajectory of the book, Matthew 25:31–46 would set the stage for the closing mandate to go to all the world (28:16–20). In his epistles, Paul often refers to the many hardships in his travels, and the apostle commends those who receive him graciously (e.g., 1 Cor. 16:5–9; Gal. 4:13–14) and encourages others to do the same for his fellow workers (e.g., Rom. 16:1–2; 1 Cor. 16:10–12).

Whatever the interpretative decision, whether the "least of these" refers to any needy person, any Christian, or Christian missionaries, the thrust of Jesus's words are the same: we must respond in concrete ways to the needs of someone from elsewhere. If the interpretive choice for these verses limits the reach of Jesus's reference, taking the "least of these" to refer to Christians or missionaries, other passages will extend the scope beyond that. Just as in the Old Testament, care for the outsider is a component of an expansive ethical vision that encompasses all who are disadvantaged.

Implications for Today

No direct teaching. This brief survey confirms that there is no explicit teaching on immigration in the Gospels. What this does *not* mean, however, is that there is nothing relevant to the immigration discussion to be found in the life and teachings of Jesus.

To begin with, one of the incidents mentioned in the Gospels about the childhood of Jesus narrates when he and his family were refugees. They fled to another country for safety. This account, like migration stories in the Old Testament, provides a point of special connection with the text to those who have had to emigrate from their homeland. Aspects of their own situation and experiences are analogous to the details of this story of Jesus.[18] Sometimes those who have been able to live stable lives and pursue careers and raise their families in peace and comfort in one place may not be able to sense the power of this account of Jesus in the same way.

Depending on one's understanding of the "stranger" and the separation of the sheep and the goats at the final judgment in Matthew 25, one might argue that the passage does not apply to the topic of immigration. At second glance, however, an important minimum admonition is apparent. As was mentioned in the introduction to this book, within several immigrant communities—those who have been here for generations as well as more recent arrivals, whether documented or undocumented—there are millions of Christians. I do not need to make a one-to-one correspondence between the disciples of Matthew 25 and all believing immigrants, yet it does seem to me that caring for fellow disciples as Jesus demands is pertinent. Many believers who come as immigrants are needy. Does the Christian church of the host culture not have a responsibility to help the "least of these" in the name of Jesus? Does not Christ dwell among these people and in them too? The text does say that Jesus is embodied in these strangers and that the judgment meted out to the nations is based in part on their treatment of disciples. Does this revelation have any application to the United States? Will the Son of

Man and the Father in any way demand an accounting for this country's actions toward Christian immigrants? Of course, if the reference to the "least of these" is wider than fellow Christians, then the relevance to our current immigration situation is much more direct. To care for these outsiders, as well as the others that are listed, is God's universal demand.

Encountering the outsider. Amid immigration discussions there is much we can glean from the way Jesus deals with Samaritans, both in his personal ministry and in his teaching. The Samaritans were culturally different from the Jews; they were despised and discriminated against. Jesus turns these attitudes on their head by intentionally having direct contact with Samaritans (one a woman and the other a leper) and using a Samaritan as the main character in a parable. In these passages, Samaritans are models of genuine relationship with God. Jesus does and says these things as a member of the majority culture of his time and place.

A key issue today concerns how the majority culture in the United States perceives national identity and its maintenance in light of the growing presence of immigrants, refugees, and asylees from Latin America and elsewhere. This is a natural concern. Jesus directly confronts the identity question through what he says and does with Samaritans. Even as he continues to live as a Jew, Jesus lays aside his culture's exclusionary mores and negative feelings toward Samaritans. Jesus chooses what is more important: the Samaritans' value as persons and the potential of their faith. Jesus gives worth, hope, and direction to a woman who has had a rough life; he heals a leper and brings him joy and a future.

Jesus's actions and attitudes transcend cultural identity; they also help define what it means to be his follower. This is not to deny the many contributions of one's own culture or the importance of a specific identity, but it does put these concerns into perspective. Perhaps these things need to be held a bit more loosely in order to feel freer to relate to people from other backgrounds. Of course, these same comments can also be directed at immigrant groups and neighborhoods. They also wrestle with maintaining what they hold most dear about their own culture in a new setting, even as they try to figure out how to negotiate the constant challenge to change at home, school, and work. All of us must learn from Jesus.

The bigger picture. Jesus's treatment of the Samaritans is but one piece of a larger set of ethical commitments. He reaches out to the poor, the sick, women, sinners of all kinds, gentiles, and Samaritans. In light of this truth, fundamental questions must be asked. What relevance is there for Christians today in what Jesus did and said? Is he simply our Savior, one to whom we turn in faith for eternal redemption? Or, in addition to our personal salvation, is his life a model for how his followers are to live in a way that pleases God and reflects his character on earth? In a sense, we are returning to the dialogue between the Jewish scribe and Jesus. What does God require of those who claim to be believers?

If the life and words of Jesus are in some fashion important and binding on Christians, then other questions naturally follow. Do we, as Christians, have as comprehensive an ethic as Jesus had? If not, why not? What areas of our life in the world have been left out, consciously or unconsciously? Have attitudes and actions toward immigrants and refugees been integrated into our Christian ethic? Along with what are normally highlighted as Christian duties—such as honesty in the workplace, fidelity in marriage, and good stewardship of money—must also stand compassion toward the outsider.

These next two sections are briefer than this one on the Gospels. The first section below looks at the use of sojourner vocabulary in the First Epistle of Peter, and the one that follows revisits the theme of hospitality.

Christians as Sojourners

Christians in Diaspora

The Greek terminology for the sojourner[19] appears several times in the First Epistle of Peter. The recipients of the letter are called "exiles" (or "strangers"; *parepidēmos*) in 1:1, and "foreigners" (*paroikos*) and "exiles" (*parepidēmos*) in 2:11 (cf. 1:17). In the Greco-Roman world, these words referred to outsiders who had moved into an area to reside there, perhaps by force or of their own volition. An "exile" (or "stranger") was a more transient resident than was the "foreigner." These outsiders were not granted the rights and privileges of full citizenship, so they lived with economic, political, and social limitations. Because they were different, they were not always welcome in their new context.[20] Some scholars understand the labels in 1 Peter to refer at some level to the sociopolitical status of the believers who received this letter. Their conversion to the Christian faith would have added spiritual difference to their civic foreignness.

The combination "foreigners and exiles" in 1 Peter 2:11 appears twice in the Septuagint, and one of these is in a very significant place: Genesis 23:4 (the other verse is Ps. 39:12 [38:13 in LXX]). In this Genesis passage, Abraham buys land to bury his wife, Sarah. This Old Testament allusion connects the experience of the addressees of this letter (and thus all believers) to the ancient patriarch. In other words, their sojourning is not unique. The history of the people of God always has been (or should be) a pilgrimage of faith while alienated from the world. Abraham's sojourning was literal and spiritual. He was an outsider, without land or roots, and he followed another God.

It is hard to know whether these Christians were sojourners in the Greco-Roman sociopolitical sense or whether these terms are metaphors describing the discrimination that believers in a general sense were suffering.[21] If actual contextual experiences within the Roman Empire determined the choice of these words, they would have had quite an impact. The Christians who read (or had read to them) this epistle from Peter were exiles in every sense of the word, literally and figuratively. Unquestionably, too, they would have been outsiders in that world simply because of their distinct lifestyle and their allegiance to Jesus. Their spiritual life yielded a different social life, one criticized by their neighbors. The letter repeatedly exhorts its readers to endure persecution with joyous confidence in the sovereignty of God and in the sure inheritance that awaits them (1:3–9; 5:10). They have been chosen by God (1:1; 2:4, 6, 9; 5:13), a standing that serves to assure them of divine care and remind them that they are different from others in that context. Theirs was to be a life of holiness, humility, constancy, and integrity, being careful not to be conformed to their surroundings during the time of their exile (1:17; cf. 1:13–14; 2:11; 4:1–11). Though they might be ostracized because of their legal status and spiritual convictions, they must maintain a good testimony. Those around them would be surprised by and oppose the Christian lifestyle (3:13–17; 4:3–5, 12–19; 5:9), but some would acknowledge the true God (2:12, 15; 3:1–2, 16).

These terms are applied to all Christians elsewhere in the New Testament, notably in the book of Hebrews, chapter 11.[22] This chapter teaches its readers that they stand in continuity with the heroes of the faith (11:4–38). Those faithful individuals willingly acknowledged that they were "strangers" (*xenos*) and "exiles" (*parepidēmos*) during their time on this earth (11:13; cf. 11:14–15, 25–26). All were steadfast through trials and tribulations as they looked forward to another place, the heavenly city (11:10, 16, 39–40). Christians are exhorted to take up this honored mantle of strangeness and to shed anything that would encumber their own journey (12:2) to the heavenly Jerusalem (12:18–24). The calling to live as foreigners and the lifelong pilgrimage to that city mean that Christians join Jesus outside the camp: in his harsh marginalization, as he hung on a cross outside the gates of the earthly Jerusalem, Jesus secured redemption (13:13–14). This orientation to the world has consequences for the life of the Christian community. The shared identity of *otherness* should generate compassion, purity, generosity (13:3–7)—and hospitality toward the stranger (13:1).

The apostle Paul also points believers to a heavenly goal, where their ultimate citizenship lies (Phil. 3:20). He uses the language of being foreigners with a different thrust, however, in the book of Ephesians. He says that in the past Christians were separated from the people of God as "strangers" (*xenos*) and "aliens" (*paroikos*),[23] but now they have been brought into the household of faith through faith in Christ (Eph. 2:12, 19).

If we return to the First Epistle of Peter, specifically to its opening verse, we see that it is addressed to God's elect, "exiles scattered" (*parepidēmois diasporas*; literally, "exiles of the diaspora" [note the addressees of James 1:1]).[24] Although this letter is addressed to a particular group of believers, the image of diaspora fits the early church generally. This is first hinted at in Acts 1:8, where the disciples are told that they will be empowered to be Jesus's witnesses in an ever-widening circle from Jerusalem to the rest of the world (cf. Matt. 28:18–20). That movement begins when some are forced out of Jerusalem and scattered by persecution (Acts 8:1–8; 11:19–30). In the providence of God, diaspora Christians become key figures in Paul's church-planting strategy. One could mention, among others, Priscilla and Aquila (18:1–2) and Apollos (18:24). Paul himself was a diaspora Jew from Tarsus and a Roman citizen. In addition, the apostle's church-planting strategy involved visiting the synagogues of diaspora Jewish communities around the Mediterranean basin (Pisidian Antioch in Acts 13; Iconium in Acts 14; Thessalonica, Berea, and Athens in Acts 17; Corinth and Ephesus in Acts 18–19). It is no surprise, therefore, that the early church was multiethnic, a point we will come back to in the discussion of hospitality (below). Diaspora and its entailments, in other words, are part of the church's DNA.

Defining Christian identity as being strangers and sojourners in the world continued into the early centuries of the church. For example, the salutation of the First Epistle of Clement, mentioned in chapter 1 (above), begins with, "The church of God which sojourns at Rome, to the church of God sojourning at Corinth . . ." A lengthy discourse about Christians appears in the Epistle of Mathetes to Diognetus, an anonymous piece from the late second century. Note the language of outsiders to describe Christians:

[5.5] They live in their own homelands, but as resident aliens [*paroikoi*]; they participate in all things as citizens [*politai*], but endure all things as strangers [*xenoi*]. Every foreign country [*xenē*] is their homeland, but every homeland is a foreign country. . . . [5.9] They spend their time on earth, but they have their citizenship [*politeuontai*] in heaven. . . . [5.17] They are opposed by the Jews as aliens [*allophyloi*], and they are persecuted by the Greeks, and those who hate them are not able to say what the reason for their hatred is. . . . [6.8] The soul which is immortal dwells in its mortal habitation, and Christians sojourn [*paroikousin*] among perishable things, while they look forward to the incorruptibility which is in heaven.[25]

The biblical story line, from beginning to end, is of God's people on the move, living as strangers—whether literally or metaphorically—in the lands where they find themselves. In all of this, across the ages and around the globe, God has accompanied his people. We might even consider that one way of speaking about God is to describe him as *Deus Migrator*.[26] If we were to press this concept further, one could interpret the incarnation as a divine migration. The Second Person of the Trinity crossed a boundary to take on human flesh as a first-century Jew in Palestine and for a time "made his dwelling" (*eskēnōsen*; literally, "encamped") among us (John 1:14). His ministry was that of an itinerant prophet, engaging all kinds of individuals on the margins and inviting them—along with everyone else—into the community of the redeemed. The church is called to do the same.

Implications for Today

There are at least three lessons that the appropriation of sojourner language in the New Testament can offer Christians engaged in the immigration discussion. The first and most important is to grasp that migration is *an important metaphor* for what it means to be a Christian. In fact, this metaphor was prominent in the thinking of the early church. The early Christians knew what it meant to be different within their imperial context, and they readily embraced the label "foreigner," "sojourner," or "stranger." This self-understanding has been a prominent mind-set across the centuries and across the breadth of theological traditions for individual Christians and the church more broadly. A well-known example is reflected in the title of the devotional classic by John Bunyan, *The Pilgrim's Progress* (1678). More recently, at the ecumenical council known as Vatican II, the Roman Catholic Church promulgated the dogmatic constitution *Lumen Gentium* (1964) that presents Christians (specifically the Catholic Church) as a pilgrim people (§§ 48–51).[27] At this juncture, the popular works cited in chapter 1 that compare the Christian life and the church to living in exile are relevant. These, too, appreciate that the church, in diverse ways, is an alien presence in the world.

Sadly, many Christians today no longer feel like "strangers in a strange land." For these Christians, this country and its culture have lost their strangeness, and they join others in wanting to keep strangers out. Perhaps it is needful to understand anew the strangeness that should mark Christian identity in the world.

This is where foreign believers in our midst can be helpful. They can remind native-born Christians of what it means to be an outsider and to carry that label wherever they go, in all their relationships, in their education, and at work. They are strangers in a physical, cultural, and social sense and have had occasion to deal with suspicion, rejection, and discrimination. Immigrant believers might identify with details of these biblical texts and read them through the lens of their analogous experiences in ways that others do not. Perhaps, then, in the grace and sovereignty of God, these foreign Christians from other countries can teach the "old ways" to the broader church! Could it even be said that, if migration is a central metaphor for the faith, the more we understand about migration and get to know immigrants, the more we might be able to recover fundamental aspects of the faith? Sometimes when I speak to Hispanic congregations, I tell them, "La iglesia de la cultura mayoritaria nos necesita" (the majority culture church needs us).

The second lesson follows from the first. If native-born Christians do embrace the immigrant, refugee, or asylee, it could mark them as civic strangers in that they would be going against the current of a good portion of public opinion. To take that stand on the basis of biblical convictions may lead to opposition from the broader culture. According to 1 Peter, though, to suffer for doing good is a privilege and part of the pilgrimage of faith.

A third takeaway is the challenge to enlarge the vision of the life and mission of the church. The New Testament church and the church of the first centuries of this era had a diasporic character and strategy. Today many are unaware that these two features increasingly characterize the global church in fresh ways. A dimension that is often missed in discussions of migration is its impact on Christian mission. On the one hand, the massive movement of populations has resulted in non-Christian individuals and groups for the first time hearing the gospel and becoming involved with churches in their new lands, something that may never have happened without migration. One could say that foreign mission fields are arriving at our doorstep. At the same time, recently arrived foreign Christians are planting churches and evangelizing their countrymen and others in their new contexts too. These rich and complex realities have given rise to what is called "diaspora missiology." Many of the leading voices in this trend are non-Western; key leaders, for instance, come from Asia. This new reality should impel Christians to connect migration to mission, to what God would have the church do in these days, whether as members of host cultures or as believing migrants in new places.[28]

In this country, immigrant churches and ministries are growing larger and multiplying. They are revitalizing Protestant denominations and the Catholic Church. These churches, in turn, are launching training schemes to prepare leaders, organizing conferences, and publishing literature that targets these groups. Multiethnic congregations are being born, and they are writing a new chapter in church history. What we are witnessing in the United States is an amazing worldwide phenomenon, a fresh and unexpected work of the Spirit that is changing the face of Christianity. Yet in many ways this is nothing new. To know the history of the church is to be aware that the church has always been on the move. In the divine plan for human history, church life and our God are connected with migration.[29]

The Call to Hospitality

New Testament Teaching

Chapter 2, the second part of our survey of the Old Testament, began with a discussion of hospitality in the ancient world and Israel. In the New Testament, hospitality also is a prominent theme. Members of the early church often shared meals and provided shelter to Christians and non-Christians, to friends, family, and strangers.[30]

Jesus himself models an attitude of generous hospitality at meals, and this to such an extent that many were scandalized. The Gospel of Luke depicts Jesus as eating in the homes of tax collectors (5:27–32; 19:1–10) and with women (10:38–42). He welcomes the repentant gesture of a sinful woman at a meal in the home of Simon the Pharisee (7:34–50) and heals a sick man in the house of another religious leader (14:1–6). When Jesus sees how guests at this dinner vie for places of prominence, he tells his host that the special invitees at a banquet in God's sight would be the poor and the sick, those of no social standing, people who would not have the means to repay the gesture (14:12–14). It is noteworthy that the parables of the lost sheep, the lost coin, and the prodigal son follow this meal (15:3–32); they are a response to the criticisms of his eating with sinners (15:1–2). Jesus, of course, is the host who miraculously feeds five thousand (9:10–17). His last meal with his disciples is a powerful gesture of intimate hospitality (22:7–38). At that dinner, Jesus mentions a future eschatological meal that will be prepared for them (22:29–30). A closing revelatory act in this Gospel is the meal Jesus shares with the disciples he met on the road to Emmaus (24:28–31). The theme of openhanded hospitality continues in Luke's second volume, the book of Acts, where it is a hallmark of the nascent Christian community (2:42–47; 4:32–35). The Gospel of Luke also shows the flip side: those who reject Jesus are characterized by a lack of hospitality (7:39; 9:51–56; 11:38, 42–54; 14:1–6).

In sum, Jesus is the paradigm of hospitality. Other Gospels extend this picture of divine hospitality. For example, at the Last Supper in the Gospel of John, Jesus goes beyond anything a host in his culture would have done by washing his disciples' feet and mandates that his disciples follow his example (13:4–20); he offers living water to the Samaritan woman at the well (4:1–45), the bread of life to the hungry (6:22–59), and a heavenly home to his followers (14:1–6).

It is to be expected, then, that Christians imitate their Lord and offer a gracious welcome to others. Accordingly, we see passages like Romans 12:13; 14:1; 15:7, 22–25; 16:1–2; 1 Corinthians 16:5–18; Colossians 4:10; Philemon 16–18; and 3 John 5–8. Importantly, the virtue of hospitality was a requirement for leadership in the Christian community (1 Tim. 3:2; Titus 1:8; cf. 1 Tim. 5:9–10). This compassionate stance was to be extended even to enemies (Rom. 12:20–21)!

The early church gathered in homes to enjoy fellowship, meet one another's physical needs, and share meals. These small assemblies were an ideal setting for practicing hospitality. The most profound opportunity to embody hospitality certainly was and continues to be the celebration of the Lord's Supper. This meal commemorates the sacrifice of Jesus on the cross and is based on his final meal with the disciples (Matt. 26:17–29 parr.). If hospitality is about opening oneself up and giving oneself to others, if it should be a time of sharing with all who claim the faith with the full expectation of God's provision, then the conjunction of the Lord's Supper and the cross is a powerful demonstration of divine hospitality. All are welcome. We who once were enemies of God have been reconciled to him and have been baptized into one body; all stand as equals before the Lord (Rom. 5:10; 1 Cor. 12:12–13; Gal. 3:27–29; Eph. 2). At the Communion table, forgiven sinners embrace other sinners and forgive those who have committed transgressions against them (cf. Matt. 6:12; Luke 11:4). It is no wonder that Paul's instruction on the Lord's Supper in 1 Corinthians 11 combines concern for the outcasts and the unfortunate with the call to serious self-evaluation (11:17–34). The Lord's Supper, so central a symbol of the Christian faith and so important for nurturing the remembrance of the person and work of Jesus, was inseparable from the practice of hospitality.

The early church was quite diverse in gender, social status, and ethnicity. Yet this diversity does not diminish the fact that such blending of all kinds of people from all kinds of places could be quite a challenge! The epistles document how these differences were playing themselves out in local assemblies. A big step in the church's transition to a multicultural and multinational entity were the experiences of the apostle Peter (Acts 10:1–11:18) and the deliberations at the Jerusalem Council (Acts 15). We see examples of ethnic and cultural tensions in the issues related to caring for Jewish and Greek widows in Jerusalem (Acts 6:1–6) and Peter's refusal to eat with Gentiles, which drew Paul's rebuke (Gal. 2:11–14). We notice the powerful statement that in Jesus the wall of separation between Jew and Gentile has come down (Eph. 2:14–22). In contrast to these initial difficulties were settings where difference was part of the social fabric, such as in Antioch, where the church leadership reflected various nationalities and ethnic backgrounds (Acts 13:1–3). One day this richness will be manifest in the heavens, where "a great multitude that no one could number, from every nation, from all tribes and peoples and languages" will gather to worship around the throne of God and the Lamb (Rev. 7:9).

Implications for Today

The New Testament reinforces the importance and value of hospitality, especially in accord with what Jesus said and did. If we claim to be followers of Jesus, how can we refuse to practice that kind of welcome with those who are different and marginalized in society? Today those outsiders include immigrants, refugees, and asylees, however they may have come. The numerous directives in the epistles make this fundamental demand even more explicit for all Christians, especially the leadership.

Of course, the Lord's Supper should be the consummate demonstration of hospitality to others, especially to the stranger in our midst. At the Lord's Table, questions of origin, language, or legal status are superseded by the embrace of friends and family and fellow believers. Here is a visible expression and public declaration of the mercy and provision of God; we all come to partake of the bread and cup as sinners before God and in need of grace.[31] To come periodically to the table without a commitment to kindness and openness to others contradicts the purpose and spirit of communing. Remember that Paul connects the practice of the Lord's Table with ethical demands that do not allow for discrimination. At the very least, the recognition of our sinfulness and of the boundless forgiveness of God should soften Christian attitudes toward outsiders in need—even those who might be undocumented immigrants.

This orientation in attitude does not solve the national legal quandary, but it can impact the direction of the conversation and its tone in ways that resonate with this most important Christian practice. At least it should transform how immigrants and refugees are discussed within the church and how the church concretely can be a beacon of hospitality to the outsider within a society that sometimes can be unwelcoming.

What about Romans 13?

Why Romans 13 Now?

I have placed this New Testament text last by design. As I travel and speak on immigration, Romans 13:1–7 is often brought up to argue against allowing entry to undocumented immigrants, or even to immigrants, refugees, and asylees more generally. The reasons given include their potential negative impact on society, the economy, and culture. In terms of the undocumented, crossing the border without proper permission and without following established policies is breaking the law of the United States. Their presence in this country by definition, therefore, is illegal. In its crassest form, I have heard this as, "What is it about 'illegal' that you don't understand?" This violation of the country's laws should be penalized, it is said, and these individuals should expect to suffer the consequences. Moreover, how can undocumented immigrants who claim to be Christians blatantly disobey a clear teaching of Scripture?

If one begins the immigration discussion with this passage, any sensible discussion about immigration is quickly aborted. Either one has proper documentation or not; one does or does not go through authorized channels, no matter what that actually entails. Everything is trumped by legal status. It is my conviction, however, that prior considerations must be dealt with before introducing issues of legality. That is why this book looks at the breadth of biblical material on migration before engaging this passage. Of course, one must treat legal matters, but at an appropriate place in the discussion. The country does need to make decisions on these issues and pass sensible legislation. Responses to the challenges of immigration, though, should arise from a set of beliefs, values, and commitments. For Christians, these values must ultimately be grounded in the full revelation found in the Bible.

If one begins with a biblical orientation that includes the centrality of the importance of the immigrant as made in the image of God, if one can appreciate how pervasive migration experiences are to the history and faith of the people of God in both Testaments, if Old Testament law projects an ethics of compassion, if the thrust of Jesus's ministry and the New Testament as a whole is to love the outsider and be hospitable, if the history and mission of the church has been built on migration, then the inclination should be to be charitable to the immigrant in the name of God and Christ. This charitable inclination, in turn, will affect how one assesses present legislation and considers where things should go from here at a personal level, within the local and national church and other Christian spheres, and finally throughout the country in law and government. The tone of the conversation will be different and the activity generated at every level will be affected, as will the kind of legislation that is brought forward or supported.

If Christians believe that current or proposed immigration legislation does not fit the teaching of the Bible and the ethical demands of God's heart, some of them will not ask, "What is it about 'illegal' that you don't understand?" Instead, they will ask, "What is it about the Bible that you do not understand?" In other words, can a Christian stance on immigration ignore the vast material in both Testaments concerning the outsider and be reduced simply to the issue of legal standing or economics or other social concerns? Again, these cannot be ignored or minimized! It is rather the question of how to approach such matters: what values will be the guiding principles within the walls of churches and in the public square?

Before these statements raise alarms, let me be clear that I am not advocating disregard of immigration law or massive civil disobedience, just as most Christians with strong misgivings about undocumented immigrants are not lobbying for a national deportation operation to rid the country of one and all. It is a narrow understanding of the nature of law and Christians' relationship to human government that I question.

Problems with Defaulting to Romans 13

Many Christians read Romans 13 with the unconscious assumption that the nation's laws are inherently good and just. The sentiment is that to obey them is not only pleasing to God but it is also common sense. We are a nation that believes in the "rule of law"!

At one level, this statement is a truism. Every nation in the history of the world has had a set of laws. We can go back thousands of years and find ancient law codes. In fact, chapter 2 looked at one such law code, that of ancient Israel. Every country on the planet today has a system of laws and, specifically, immigration laws. It is not enough, therefore, to simply declare that the United States follows a "rule of law." Rather, the deeper issue to consider is whether the legal system that is currently in place is good (in relationship to our Christian commitments) and practical and efficient (for the national good). In light of what has been presented in this book, I argue that current immigration law is found wanting.

All sides of the debate recognize the inadequacy of the current immigration law. Most who defend current legislation are unaware of its history and requirements and of how it functions (e.g., on a set of outdated quotas of multiple kinds). There are differences as to the nature of proposed solutions, which range from being exclusionary and punitive to being welcoming and gracious. And, contrary to the caricature, to opt for being welcoming and gracious is not to advocate for open borders and no restrictions (although there are those who do argue for such things). It is, however, to reimagine the nature and purpose of immigration legislation in greater conformity to biblical principles.

The need to begin with Romans 12. Romans 12 sets the stage for Paul's words concerning human government in chapter 13. It contrasts the mind-set and life of Christians with what they encounter in society. Romans 12 exhorts believers not to be molded by the "pattern of this world" (12:1–2). This includes being shaped by political ideologies—in this case, going along with what one's political party says about immigration and the treatment of immigrants. Instead, Christians should have their minds renewed through the Scripture so that they might know the will of God. This renewal of the mind concerning immigration has been the purpose of this book.

Paul goes on to say that believers should humbly serve others, have compassion, and strive to live peaceably with everyone (12:3–18). He closes this section with a radical exhortation: we are to feed and give drink even to our enemies (12:19–21; cf. Matt. 5:43–48; Luke 6:27–36). This is a strong word to those who are suspicious of certain immigrants, refugees, and asylees. The lesson is this: even if immigrants are perceived to be "enemies," Christians are called to care for their needs. Indeed, current immigration law does not prohibit charitable outreach to foreigners, even those who are undocumented. English-learning classes, food and clothes pantries, after-school tutoring, recreational opportunities, legal aid, and much more are permitted under current legislation. A host of ministries and initiatives are working in these areas.

Discerning submission, not blind obedience. With this backdrop and an awareness of what has been covered in this book, we turn to Romans 13. First, the government is an institution different from the church. It has a different agenda, a different reason for existence, and different values and rules. How does the set of commitments in Romans 12 carry over to living in society under these conditions? Christians, Paul says, should respect the government. The text says, "Be subject" (or "submit," *hypotassō*) to the established authorities (13:1). It does not say "obey." In other words, our appreciation of what any government pronounces or enacts will have boundaries (note the apostles' statement in Acts 4:19–20). This respect does not mean agreeing with or sanctifying everything a human government says and does. If one does not follow a law, there may be a sanction to which one must submit. The reason is that Christians respond to a higher authority, to the Lord of the church (Matt. 28:18; Eph. 1:20–23; Phil. 2:9–11; Col. 1:15–18; Rev. 1:17–18; etc.), and thus to a higher law and set of values. There will be times when these two authorities will not agree. How to adjudicate or settle matters on these issues has occupied Christian theology for centuries.[32]

The political system of the United States allows the wonderful privilege of the right to disagree with the government and to change laws that are deemed inadequate, dated, or unjust. Motivated by their principles, Christians exercise their civil rights all the time in multiple ways: at the ballot box; through publications; by organizing educational, legal, and civic organizations that defend certain points of view; by participating peacefully in advocacy for a host of causes. I could go on. Each of these actions in its own way expresses reservations about the way things are and the matters that the government mandates.

This is the history of politics in this country. One powerful example was the overturning of segregation laws through the efforts of the civil rights movement. Such changes are difficult and can be painful and chaotic; they generate debates and reveal conflicting agendas. That is the nature of life in a democracy. The United States Congress recognizes that it must change its immigration legislation, even though people understand what that entails in diverse ways. The national leadership across the political spectrum and the country as a whole are aware that the immigration regulations now in place are not working and must be revised or replaced. The numbers arriving at the southern border are becoming unmanageable under current laws; disorder and suffering follow (and this is a reality at borders in various countries around the world).

In sum, to quote Romans 13 on the immigration issue without nuance or biblical and historical depth simply will not do. Christians should search the Scriptures for guidance in evaluating the development of immigration policy and engaging its multifaceted set of problems. From that foundation, Christians could begin moving forward to consider legal issues. Discussion on legality and possible structural alternatives cannot be limited to complying with the present laws and remaining with the status quo. If the laws are problematic theologically, humanely, and pragmatically—and everyone agrees that some sort of reform is needed—the call in Romans 13 to submit to the authorities can be processed in fresh and constructive ways. Respect for the nation's present laws is then coupled with and informed by a move toward a new set of laws. As Christians participate in this change, in whatever fashion, they should do so self-consciously *as Christians*.

Immigrants and Romans 13

Here I offer some observations concerning how Hispanic believers who are undocumented immigrants respond to Romans 13. Of course, there would be some who set aside the passage on exegetical, theological, and pastoral grounds. My experience, however, is with Hispanic Christians primarily of the evangelical and Pentecostal streams. They take this biblical text seriously, but their view is complex.

These Christians recognize that they are in violation of current law by living and working here. At the same time, they have experienced personally the law's contradictions and inequities. For example, the government turns a blind eye to many employers who hire undocumented workers because the country needs cheap labor for harvesting its food, for construction and landscaping, and for other so-called unskilled jobs. At the same time, it closes the door to social services for these same workers. Immigrants also respect the legal system of the United States for its efficiency and fairness in many areas. Many pay taxes, and they do their best to obey the laws of the land in every area that does not threaten their jobs, homes, daily lives, and children's education. I have heard many express a desire to be model "citizens" as part of their Christian duty and in order to gain the respect of the majority culture. Finally, all wish for a legal resolution of the situation. Their hope is that the law itself will be reformed in such a way that their legal status is no longer an issue and that they might live peacefully in their new land and contribute to society.

Conclusion

For Christians, the ultimate standard for understanding our world and for living out all dimensions of daily life is the person of Jesus Christ. This chapter argues that his teaching and his attitudes and actions toward others must serve as the foundational orientation for how we engage vulnerable outsiders who have come seeking a new life. Jesus Christ's stance of welcoming the marginalized and the Other is carried on throughout the New Testament. It characterized the multiethnic and international congregations that made up the early church. These interactions were difficult, both in the ministry of Jesus and within those first fledgling groups of believers, but the early Christians grasped that this human complexity was God's design for his people.

This new creation called the church is odd to the world. That is why the New Testament's characterization of Christians as strangers and exiles is fitting. As believers, we are constantly challenged to live into that calling in every part of our personal and social lives. Accordingly, we must engage debates on immigration and refugee and asylee resettlement through a biblical lens. Objective socioeconomic analysis, realistic policy suggestions, and sensitive cultural arguments clearly are necessary, yet for the Christian, these discussions should be commensurate with the values and commitments that are grounded in Jesus and the New Testament.

Epilogue

The Scriptures and the Future

The title of this epilogue sums up the concern of this book: How will the Scriptures shape the position taken by Christians, individually and corporately, on the topic of immigration? My hope is that this volume demonstrates that there is a consistent ethic of hospitable welcome toward the outsider across both Testaments. Christian traditions regularly affirm that the Bible is foundational for faith and practice, but living out this conviction well is a never-ending challenge.

The amount of narrative, legal, and epistolary material in the Bible that deals with migration in some form or fashion is impressive. We began with the image of God in the first chapter of Genesis and various stories of migration in that book. Then we traced many other accounts of migration experiences in the Old Testament, coupled with noticing the array of laws favoring the outsider in the Pentateuch. A reader cannot help but be aware of how central the theme of migration is to the Old Testament. The New Testament reinforces such observations through the life and teachings of Jesus and the perspectives and strategies of the early church. The first Christians also defined themselves as a community of strangers in the world: the migration metaphor was a fitting description of their earthly pilgrimage.

The current immigration debate is timely not only for the global community of nations but also for *Christians* and the *church*. The issues revolving around migration and the growing presence of immigrants and refugees in this country and elsewhere serve to remind all believers and ecclesial bodies of the most basic demands of our faith: compassion, the mission to be a blessing to outsiders and to the broader society, and the call to imitate Christ, even if that stance might contradict certain political ideologies or cultural habits. That is, urgent immigration realities can force Christians to take a self-conscious stand on scriptural revelation, no matter what others may say and irrespective of the volatility of the topic. Immigration provides the opportunity to bear a clear witness to some of the ethical tenets of the Christian faith that are so strongly grounded in the Bible.

This commitment requires reading the Bible virtuously—that is, reading in such a way that one progressively becomes the kind of person the Scriptures were designed to shape.[1] As individual Christians and churches grow into this vision, they can embrace the Other. Jesus has brought us—who once were far off—into the family of God (Rom. 5:10; Eph. 2:12–13). This is an existential fact for all Christians that can echo the tangible lived experiences of millions who arrive from other lands. It is time to embrace this difficult historical moment, return to the Bible, and do the necessary and creative theological and pastoral work to respond in faithfulness to today's challenges.

Repeatedly in the Bible, God's people are strongly admonished if there is a disconnect between care for the vulnerable and worship. Whether the prophets are railing against unacceptable rituals in the temple (e.g., Isa. 1:10–20; 58; Jer. 7:1–15; Amos 5:21–24; Mic. 6:1–8; Zech. 7:8–10; cf. Pss. 15, 24) or Jesus is denouncing a Sabbath divorced from mercy (e.g., Matt. 12:1–14 parr.) or Paul and James are rebuking callous favoritism at worship services (1 Cor. 11:17–34; James 2:1–13), the just treatment of those in need is a criterion for devotion pleasing to God. The ethical matters connected to immigration, immigrants, refugees, and asylees need to be considered under this rubric so that Christian homes and churches might stand as moral beacons in a confusing and sometimes cruel world.

Debates in the coming years will not be easy, and the political and policy choices will be complex. The Scriptures, however, communicate a clear mandate to embrace the stranger. May God grant us the wisdom and discernment to fulfill that call faithfully.

Notes

Introduction

1. For these data and links to resources, see https://www.unhcr.org.
2. The International Organization for Migration: https://www.iom.int. Also note organizations such as the Refugee Studies Centre in Oxford, UK: https://www.rsc.ox.ac.uk/research.
3. Pew Research Center: https://www.pewresearch.org/; Migration Policy Institute: https://www.migrationpolicy.org/; the Department of Homeland Security: https://www.dhs.gov/immigration-statistics.
4. The Roman Catholic Church has a long tradition of dealing with migration and immigrants. For a survey of Catholic documents, see Carmen M. Nanko-Fernández, "A Documented Response: Papal Teaching and People on the Move," in *Immigrant Neighbors among Us: Immigration across Theological Traditions*, ed. M. D. Carroll R. and L. A. Sánchez M. (Eugene, OR: Pickwick, 2015), 1–21. Other Catholic sources include the Missionaries of St. Charles Borromeo (or Scalabrinian Missionaries) and the Center for Migration Studies (https://cmsny.org). Also note *Immigrants among Us: A Lutheran Framework for Addressing Immigration Issues* (St. Louis: Lutheran Church—Missouri Synod, 2012). Other denominational statements, including those of the Southern Baptist Convention (and its Ethics & Religious Liberty Commission), the Presbyterian Church (USA), the Wesleyan Church, among others, are available online.
5. An incredible number could be mentioned, including Daniel C. Groody, *Border of Death, Valley of Life: An Immigrant Journey of Heart and Spirit*, Celebrating Faith: Explorations in Latino Spirituality and Theology (Lanham, MD: Rowman & Littlefield, 2002); Robert W. Heimburger, *God and the Illegal Alien: United States Immigration Law and a Theology of Politics*,

Cambridge Studies in Law and Christianity (Cambridge: Cambridge University Press, 2018); Carroll R. and Sánchez M., *Immigrant Neighbors among Us*. For a more restrictive view, see Peter C. Meilaender, *Toward a Theory of Immigration* (New York: Palgrave, 2001).

6. Full-length studies include, e.g., Great Britain: Nick Spencer, *Asylum and Immigration: A Christian Perspective on a Polarized Debate* (Milton Keynes, UK: Paternoster, 2004); Fleur S. Houston, *You Shall Love the Stranger as Yourself: The Bible, Refugees, and Asylum* (New York: Routledge, 2015); Spain: Juan Simarro Fernández, *Inmigrantes: El multiforme rostro de Dios* (Madrid: Misión Evangélica Urbana and Consejo Evangélico de Madrid, 2008); José Antonio Martínez Díez, *El cristiano ante la inmigración* (Madrid: Editorial PPC, 2008); Latin America: José E. Ramírez Kidd, *El extranjero, la viuda y el huérfano en el Antiguo Testamento* (Guatemala: CEDEPCA; San José, CR: Universidad Bíblica Latinoamericana, 2003); Elsa Tamez Luna, *Historias de migrantes de la Biblia* (Barueri, Brazil: Sociedad Bíblica de Brasil, 2015); United States: James K. Hoffmeier, *The Immigration Crisis: Immigrants, Aliens, and the Bible* (Wheaton: Crossway, 2009); Mark W. Hamilton, *Jesus, King of Strangers: What the Bible Really Says about Immigration* (Grand Rapids: Eerdmans, 2019). More technical monographs appear in the notes below. Some scholars, however, see the Bible as inherently xenophobic: e.g., Brian Rainey, *Religion, Ethnicity and Xenophobia in the Bible: A Theoretical, Exegetical and Theological Study*, Routledge Studies in the Biblical World (New York: Routledge, 2019).

7. M. Daniel Carroll R., *Christians at the Border: Immigration, the Church, and the Bible*, 2nd ed. (Grand Rapids: Brazos, 2013).

8. For a convenient list of terms, see https://www.iom.int/key-migration-terms.

9. See https://www.census.gov/prod/cen2010/briefs/c2010br-04.pdf. Another term is *Chicano* (feminine, *Chicana*). This word refers to those of Mexican descent in the United States and is sometimes associated with a more militant approach to Mexican-American ethnicity and history.

10. As examples, see Jean-Pierre Ruiz, *Readings from the Edges: The Bible and People on the Move* (Maryknoll, NY: Orbis, 2011); Francisco Lozada Jr. and Fernando F. Segovia, eds., *Latino/a Biblical Hermeneutics: Problematics, Objectives, Strategies*, SBL Semeia Studies 68 (Atlanta: SBL Press, 2014); Efraín Agosto and Jacqueline M. Hidalgo, eds., *Latinxs, the Bible, and Migration*, The Bible and Cultural Studies (New York: Palgrave Macmillan, 2018). Also see the resources listed in note 38 of chapter 1.

11. Note these books and their bibliographies: Stéphane Dufoix, *Diasporas*, trans. W. Rodarmor (Berkeley: University of California Press, 2008); Stephen Castles, Hein de Haas, and Mark J. Miller, *The Age of Migration: International Population Movements in the Modern World*, 5th ed. (New York: Guilford, 2014); Mary C. Waters, Reed Ueda, and Helen B. Marrow, eds., *The New Americans: A Guide to Immigration since 1965* (Cambridge, MA: Harvard

University Press, 2007); Elena Fiddian-Qasmiyeh et al., eds., *The Oxford Handbook of Refugee and Forced Migration Studies* (New York: Oxford University Press, 2014); Ronald H. Bayor, ed., *The Oxford Handbook of American Immigration and Ethnicity* (New York: Oxford University Press, 2016).

Chapter 1 "My Father Was a Wandering Aramean": Stories of Migration in the Old Testament

1. Scholarly resources are cited in these endnotes for those who desire to pursue details in greater depth. I also will be dealing with the canonical shape of these texts, not with scholarly reconstructions. For a discussion of such matters, see my "Ethics and Old Testament Interpretation," in *Hearing the Old Testament: Listening for God's Address*, ed. C. G. Bartholomew and J. H. Beldman (Grand Rapids: Eerdmans, 2012), 204–27.

2. J. Richard Middleton, *The Liberating Image: The* Imago Dei *in Genesis 1* (Grand Rapids: Brazos, 2005); J. Gordon McConville, *Being Humans in God's World: An Old Testament Theology of Humanity* (Grand Rapids: Baker Academic, 2016), 11–45; cf. Christopher J. H. Wright, *Old Testament Ethics for the People of God* (Downers Grove, IL: InterVarsity, 2004), 116–29; John H. Walton, *Old Testament Theology for Christians: From Ancient Context to Enduring Belief* (Downers Grove, IL: IVP Academic, 2017), 84–99; Ryan S. Peterson, *The* Imago Dei *as Human Identity: A Theological Interpretation*, Journal of Theological Interpretation Supplements 14 (Winona Lake, IN: Eisenbrauns, 2016).

3. Note the reflections in Miroslav Volf, *Exclusion and Embrace: A Theological Exploration of Identity, Otherness, and Reconciliation* (Nashville: Abingdon, 1996), 92–98.

4. Guy S. Goodwin-Gill, "The International Law of Refugee Protection," and Jane McAdam, "Human Rights and Forced Migration," in Elena Fiddian-Qasmiyeh et al., eds., *The Oxford Handbook of Refugee and Forced Migration Studies* (New York: Oxford University Press, 2014), 36–47 and 203–14, respectively.

5. Early theological reflections on *mestizaje* are Virgilio Elizondo, *Galilean Journey: The Mexican-American Promise* (Maryknoll, NY: Orbis, 1983); Justo L. González, *Santa Biblia: The Bible through Hispanic Eyes* (Nashville: Abingdon, 1996), 77–90. At a personal level, see Orlando Crespo, *Being Latino in Christ: Finding Wholeness in Your Ethnic Identity* (Downers Grove, IL: InterVarsity, 2003). Recent discussions include Néstor Medina, *Mestizaje: Remapping Race, Culture, and Faith in Latina/o Catholicism*, Studies in Latino/a Catholicism (Maryknoll, NY: Orbis, 2009); Carmen Nanko-Fernández, *Theologizing in Spanglish: Context, Community, and Ministry*, Studies in Latino/a Catholicism (Maryknoll, NY: Orbis, 2010).

6. Each of the items in this list has pastoral concerns as its root, for instance, in terms of family issues: immigrants who have left spouses and children in their home country and then have another family or partner in the

US, the incidence of alcoholism and drug use, the allure of gangs for young people, the temptation of irresponsible consumerism after coming from a more deprived background.

7. For background to the patriarchal narratives, see K. A. Kitchen, *On the Reliability of the Old Testament* (Grand Rapids: Eerdmans, 2003), 313–43; Richard S. Hess, "The Ancestral Period," in *Behind the Scenes of the Old Testament: Cultural, Social, and Historical Contexts*, ed. J. S. Greer, J. W. Hilber, and J. H. Walton (Grand Rapids: Baker Academic, 2018), 187–93. For a more skeptical view of the historical plausibility of these narratives, see Mark Elliott and J. Edward Wright, "The Book of Genesis and Israel's Ancestral Traditions," in *The Old Testament in Archaeology and History*, ed. J. Ebeling et al. (Waco: Baylor University Press, 2017), 213–32.

8. Anthony Leahy, "Ethnic Diversity in Ancient Egypt," in *Civilizations of the Ancient Near East*, ed. Jack M. Sasson (Peabody, MA: Hendrickson, 1995), 1:225–34; Kenton L. Sparks, *Ethnicity and Identity in Ancient Israel: Prolegomena to the Study of Ethnic Sentiments and Their Expression in the Hebrew Bible* (Winona Lake, IN: Eisenbrauns, 1998), 75–93; Kitchen, *On the Reliability of the Old Testament*, 343–44. See Egyptian depictions of Semites entering Egypt in James K. Hoffmeier, *The Immigration Crisis: Immigrants, Aliens, and the Bible* (Wheaton: Crossway, 2009), 39–40; *CSB Study Bible* (Nashville: Holman Bible Publishers, 2011), 29.

9. James K. Hoffmeier, *Israel in Egypt: The Evidence for the Authenticity of the Exodus Tradition* (New York: Oxford University Press, 1996), 52–76; Hoffmeier, *The Immigration Crisis*, 38–46.

10. See esp. Mark W. Hamilton, *Jesus, King of Strangers: What the Bible Really Says about Immigration* (Grand Rapids: Eerdmans, 2019), 16–27; cf. Jean-Pierre Ruiz, *Readings from the Edges: The Bible and People on the Move* (Maryknoll, NY: Orbis, 2011), 64–68.

11. Quoted in Daniel Smith-Christopher, *A Biblical Theology of Exile*, Overtures to Biblical Theology (Minneapolis: Fortress, 2002), 167.

12. For the background of Egypt in the time of Joseph, see Hoffmeier, *Israel in Egypt*, 77–106; Kitchen, *On the Reliability of the Old Testament*, 344–52. For possible reasons for Joseph's brothers not recognizing him, see Lisbeth S. Fried, "Why Did Joseph Shave?," *Biblical Archaeology Review* 33, no. 4 (2007): 36–41. Doubts concerning the historicity of the Joseph material are expressed in Elliott and Wright, "The Book of Genesis and Israel's Ancestral Traditions," 232–39.

13. For Daniel as resistance literature and political critique, see John Goldingay, "The Stories in Daniel: A Narrative Politics," *Journal for the Study of the Old Testament* 37 (1987): 99–116; Smith-Christopher, *A Biblical Theology of Exile*, 182–88; David M. Valeta, *Lions and Ovens and Visions: A Satirical Reading of Daniel 1–6*, Hebrew Bible Monographs 12 (Sheffield: Sheffield Phoenix, 2008); Anathea E. Portier-Young, *Apocalypse against Empire: Theologies of Resistance in Early Judaism* (Grand Rapids: Eerdmans, 2013), esp. 223–79;

Brennan Breed, "A Divided Tongue: The Moral Taste Buds of the Book of Daniel," *Journal for the Study of the Old Testament* 40, no. 1 (2015): 113–30.

14. Daniel L. Smith-Christopher has applied refugee, trauma, and diaspora studies to the exile in *The Religion of the Landless: The Social Context of the Exile* (Bloomington, IN: Meyer-Stone, 1989); Smith-Christopher, *A Biblical Theology of Exile*; Smith-Christopher, "Reading War and Trauma: Suggestions toward a Social-Psychological Exegesis of Exile and War in Biblical Texts"; and Frank Ritchel Ames, "The Cascading Effects of Exile: From Diminished Resources to New Identities," in *Interpreting Exile: Displacement and Deportation in Biblical and Modern Contexts*, ed. B. E. Kelle, F. R. Ames, and J. L. Wright, Ancient Israel and Its Literature (Atlanta: Society of Biblical Literature, 2011), 253–74 and 173–87, respectively.

15. For the texts of various inscriptions of the Assyrian kings Tiglath-pileser III, Sargon II, and Sennacherib, texts in which they document the invasions and occasionally provide numbers of deportees, see *The Context of Scripture*, ed. W. H. Hallo and K. L. Younger Jr., 3 vols. (Leiden: Brill, 2000), 2:284–305; Mordechai Cogan, *The Raging Torrent: Historical Inscriptions from Assyria and Babylon Relating to Ancient Israel*, 2nd ed. (Jerusalem: Carta, 2015), 54–143.

16. For a broader discussion that includes the biblical accounts, see Daniel C. Snell, *Flight and Freedom in the Ancient Near East*, Culture and History of the Ancient Near East 8 (Leiden: Brill, 2001).

17. C. A. Strine, "Your Name Shall No Longer Be Jacob, but Refugee: Insights into Gen. 25:19–33:20 from Involuntary Migration Studies," in *Scripture in Social Discourse: Social Scientific Perspectives on Early Jewish and Christian Writings*, ed. C. Strine, T. Klutz, and J. Keady (London: Bloomsbury T&T Clark, 2018), 51–69; C. A. Strine, "The Study of Involuntary Migration as a Hermeneutical Guide for Reading the Jacob Narrative," *Biblical Interpretation*, nos. 4–5 (2018): 485–98.

18. Hoffmeier, *Israel in Egypt*, 138–44; Kitchen, *On the Reliability of the Old Testament*, 295–99.

19. Aaron A. Burke, "An Anthropological Model for the Investigation of Refugees in Iron Age Judah and Its Environs," in *Interpreting Exile*, ed. Kelle, Ames, and Wright, 41–56.

20. Hoffmeier, *Israel in Egypt*, 109–22; Kitchen, *On the Reliability of the Old Testament*, 245–49. For insights into the brick laying, see Robert Littman, Marta Lorenzon, and Jay Silverstein, "With and Without Straw: How Israelite Slaves Made Bricks," *Biblical Archaeology Review* 40, no. 2 (2014): 60–63, 71.

21. Bob Becking, *The Fall of Samaria: An Historical and Archaeological Study*, Studies in the History of the Ancient Near East 11 (Leiden: Brill, 1992), 61–93; Bustaney Oded, "The Settlements of the Israelite and the Judean Exiles in Mesopotamia in the 8th–6th Centuries BCE," in *Studies in Historical Geography and Biblical Historiography Presented to Zecharia Kallai*, ed. G. Galil and M. Weinfeld, Supplements to Vetus Testamentum 452 (Leiden:

Brill, 2000), 91–103; K. Lawson Younger Jr., "'Give Us Our Daily Bread': Everyday Life for the Israelite Deportees," in *Life and Culture in the Ancient Near East*, ed. R. E. Averbeck, M. W. Chavalas, and D. B. Weisberg (Bethesda, MD: CDL Press, 2003), 269–88; Mordechai Cogan, *Bound for Exile: Israelites and Judeans under Imperial Yoke; Documents from Assyria and Babylonia* (Jerusalem: Carta, 2013), 34–53 and 118–33. The apocryphal book of Tobit is set in the Assyrian diaspora.

22. In addition to the biblical text, for more on Babylon see Laurie E. Pearce, "New Evidence for Judeans in Babylonia," in *Judah and the Judeans in the Persian Period*, ed. Oded Lipschits and Manfred Oeming (Winona Lake, IN: Eisenbrauns, 2006), 399–411; Cornelia Wunsch, "Glimpses on the Lives of Deportees in Rural Babylonia," in *Arameans, Chaldeans, and Arabs in Babylonia and Palestine in the First Millennium BC*, ed. A. Berlejung and M. P. Streck, Leipziger Altorientalistische Studien 3 (Wiesbaden: Harrassowitz, 2013), 247–60; Cogan, *Bound for Exile*, 134–57. Also note Hamilton, *Jesus, King of Strangers*, 98–111.

23. For what follows, note the observations of C. A. Strine, "Embracing Asylum and Refugees: Jeremiah 29 as Foundation for a Christian Theology of Migration and Integration," *Political Theology* 19, no. 6 (2018): 478–96; Strine, "Before and after Exile: Involuntary Migration and the Ideas of Israel," *Hebrew Bible and Ancient Israel* 7, no. 3 (2018): 289–315; Ruiz, *Readings from the Edges*, 83–99.

24. John J. Ahn, *Exile as Forced Migrations: A Sociological, Literary, and Theological Approach on the Displacement and Resettlement of the Southern Kingdom of Judah*, Beihefte zur Zeitschrift für die alttestamentliche Wissenschaft 417 (Berlin: de Gruyter, 2011); Ahn, "Forced Migrations Guiding the Exile: Demarcating 597, 587, and 582 BCE," in *By the Irrigation Canals of Babylon: Approaches to the Study of Exile*, ed. J. J. Ahm and J. Middlemas, Library of Biblical Studies/Old Testament 526 (New York: Bloomsbury T&T Clark, 2012), 173–89; cf. Bo H. Lim, "Exile and Migration: Toward a Biblical Theology of Immigration and Displacement," *Covenant Quarterly* 74, no. 2 (2016): 3–15.

25. For the queen of heaven, see Philip J. King, *Jeremiah: An Archaeological Companion* (Louisville: Westminster John Knox, 1993), 102–7; C. Houtman, "Queen of Heaven," in *Dictionary of Deities and Demons in the Bible*, ed. K. van der Toorn, B. Becking, and P. W. van der Horst, 2nd ed. (Grand Rapids: Eerdmans, 1999), 678–80.

26. For Elephantine, see Bezalel Poten, "The Jews in Egypt," in *The Cambridge History of Judaism*, ed. W. D. Davies and L. Finkelstein (Cambridge: Cambridge University Press, 1984), 1:372–400; Gard Granerød, *Dimensions of Yahwism in the Persian Period: Studies in the Religion and Society of the Judaean Community at Elephantine*, Beihefte zur Zeitschrift für die alttestamentliche Wissenschaft 488 (Berlin: De Gruyter, 2016).

27. For an accessible introduction to compositional and historical discussions, see Lena-Sofia Tiemeyer, *Ezra-Nehemiah: Israel's Quest for Identity; An Introduction and Study Guide*, T&T Clark Study Guides to the Old Testament (London: Bloomsbury T&T Clark, 2017), 39–84.

28. Some suggest that Nehemiah was given permission to build the walls of Jerusalem for imperial reasons. In this view, with the Greek threat to Persia rising, Artaxerxes commissions the project to bolster the empire's southern flank. If this is correct, then it is more evidence of Nehemiah's loyalty to Persia. The project would have benefited both the Jews and the empire.

29. Katherine E. Southwood, "The Holy Seed: The Significance of Endogamous Boundaries and Their Transgression in Ezra 9–10," in *Judah and the Judeans in the Achaemenid Period: Negotiating Identity in an International Context*, ed. O. Lipschits, G. N. Knoppers, and M. Oeming (Winona Lake, IN: Eisenbrauns, 2011), 189–223; Southwood, "'And They Could Not Understand Jewish Speech': Language, Ethnicity, and Nehemiah's Intermarriage Crisis," *Journal of Theological Studies* 62, no. 1 (2011): 1–18; Southwood, *Ethnicity and the Mixed Marriage Crisis in Ezra 9–10: An Anthropological Approach*, Oxford Theological Monographs (Oxford: Oxford University Press, 2012); cf. Christian Frevel, ed., *Mixed Marriages: Intermarriage and Group Identity in the Second Temple Period*, Library of Hebrew Bible/Old Testament Studies 547 (New York: Bloomsbury T&T Clark, 2011); cf. Tiemeyer, *Ezra-Nehemiah*, 86–95; Ruiz, *Reading from the Edges*, 100–14.

30. Jacob Neusner, "Babylonia," *Encyclopaedia Judaica*, 2nd ed. (Detroit: Macmillan, 2007), 3:24–30; Nissim Kazzaz, "Iraq," *Encyclopaedia Judaica*, 10:14–21.

31. In addition to sources mentioned above in n. 22, see Laura E. Pearce, "'Judean': A Special Status in Neo-Babylonian and Achemenid Babylonia," in *Judah and the Judeans in the Achaemenid Period: Negotiating Identity in an International Context*, ed. O. Lipschits, G. N. Knoppers, and M. Oeming (Winona Lake, IN: Eisenbrauns, 2011), 267–77; Angelika Berlejung, "Social Climbing in the Babylonian Exile," in *Wandering Arameans: Arameans outside Syria; Textual and Archaeological Perspectives*, ed. A. Berlejung, A. M. Maeir, and A. Schüle, Leipziger Altorientalistische Studien 5 (Wiesbaden: Harrassowitz, 2017), 101–24; Tero Alstola, "Judeans in Babylonia: A Study of Deportees in the Sixth and Fifth Centuries BCE" (PhD diss., University of Helsinki, 2018).

32. For these and other issues, see Edwin M. Yamauchi, *Persia and the Bible* (Grand Rapids: Baker, 1990), 226–39; Karen Jobes, *Esther*, NIV Application Commentary (Grand Rapids: Zondervan, 1999); Adele Berlin, *Esther*, JPS Bible Commentary (Philadelphia: Jewish Publication Society, 2001); Steed Vernyl Davidson, "Diversity, Difference, and Access to Power in Diaspora: The Case of the Book of Esther," *Word & World* 29, no. 3 (2009): 280–87. For details on the women in the palace, see Pierre Briant, *From Cyrus to*

Alexander: A History of the Persian Empire, trans. P. T. Daniels (Winona Lake, IN: Eisenbrauns, 2002), 277–86.

33. For details of this structure, see Joan Goodnick Westenholz, ed., *Royal Cities of the Biblical World* (Jerusalem: Bible Lands Museum, 1996), 244–46; Anthony Tomasino, "Esther," in *Zondervan Illustrated Bible Backgrounds Commentary*, ed. J. H. Walton (Grand Rapids: Zondervan, 2009), 3:485; cf. Briant, *From Cyrus to Alexander*, 259–61.

34. Elsewhere Israelites bow before superiors and kings (e.g., Gen. 23:7; 33:3; 1 Sam. 24:8; 2 Sam. 14:14), so bowing down in and of itself may not be the issue. The text's repetition that Haman was an Agagite (Esther 3:1, 10; 8:5; 9:24) might make a connection to the historic enmity between the Agagites and the Israelites (Exod. 17:8–16; Deut. 25:17–19; 1 Sam. 15:1–3) and be the reason for Mordecai's refusal.

35. Esther is the only book of the Bible that does not mention God. This caused some ancients to doubt whether it should be included in the canon. The Septuagint (the Greek translation of the Hebrew text) resolved the problem by adding over one hundred lines to the book. The additions include prayers and the insertion of the name of God.

36. Stanley Hauerwas and William H. Willimon, *Resident Aliens: Life in the Christian Colony; A Provocative Christian Assessment of Culture and Ministry for People Who Know That Something Is Wrong*, 25th anniversary ed. (Nashville: Abingdon, 2014); cf., e.g., David Kinnaman and Mark Matlock, *Faith for Exiles: 5 Ways for a New Generation to Follow Jesus in Digital Babylon* (Grand Rapids: Brazos, 2019).

37. E.g., Walter Brueggemann, *Cadences of Home: Preaching among the Exiles* (Louisville: Westminster John Knox, 1997); Brueggemann, *Out of Babylon* (Nashville: Abingdon, 2010). Also see the many appropriations of Ps. 137 in American history in David W. Stowe, *Song of Exile: The Enduring Mystery of Psalm 137* (New York: Oxford University Press, 2016).

38. E.g., Ada María Isasi-Díaz, "'By the Rivers of Babylon': Exile as a Way of Life," in *Reading from This Place: Social Location and Biblical Interpretation in Global Perspective*, ed. F. F. Segovia and M. A. Tolbert (Minneapolis: Fortress, 1995), 149–63; Fernando F. Segovia, "In the World but Not of It: Exile as a Locus for a Theology of the Diaspora," in *Hispanic/Latino Theology: Challenge and Promise*, ed. A. M. Isasi-Díaz and F. F. Segovia (Minneapolis: Fortress, 1996), 195–217; González, *Santa Biblia*, 91–102; Luis Rivera-Rodríguez, "Toward a Diaspora Hermeneutics (Hispanic North America)," in *Character Ethics and the Old Testament*, ed. M. D. Carroll R. and J. E. Lapsley (Louisville: Westminster John Knox, 2007), 169–89. Gregory Lee Cuéllar connects certain texts in Isaiah (which he dates to the postexilic period) to the experience of Mexican immigrants in *Voices of Marginality: Exile and Return in Second Isaiah 40–55 and the Mexican Immigrant Experience*, American University Studies, Series VII, vol. 271 (New York: Peter Lang, 2008).

39. Hans de Wit, *En la dispersión, el texto es patria: Introducción a la hermenéutica clásica, moderna y posmoderna* (San José, CR: Universidad Bíblica Latinoamericana, 2002).

Chapter 2 "You Are to Love Those Who Are Foreigners": Old Testament Law and the Sojourner

1. E.g., Patrick J. Buchanan, *State of Emergency: The Third World Invasion and Conquest of America* (New York: Thomas Dunne, 2006), 220–25.

2. Philip J. King and Lawrence E. Stager, *Life in Biblical Israel*, Library of Ancient Israel (Louisville: Westminster John Knox, 2001), 61–63; cf. Andrew Arterbury, *Entertaining Angels: Early Christian Hospitality in Its Mediterranean Setting*, New Testament Monographs 8 (Sheffield: Sheffield Phoenix Press, 2005), 55–93, and passim.

3. Joshua W. Jipp, *Saved by Faith and Hospitality* (Grand Rapids: Eerdmans, 2017), 127–33. I was made aware of 1 Clement in Jipp, *Saved by Faith and Hospitality*, 3–7. For 1 Clement, see Alexander Roberts and James Donaldson, eds., *The Anti-Nicene Fathers* (Grand Rapids: Eerdmans, 1989), 1:1–21.

4. Christopher J. H. Wright, *Old Testament Ethics for the People of God*, 68. His full discussion appears on 48–75, 182–211. For Deut. 4:5–8, see Christopher J. H. Wright, *Mission of God: Unlocking the Bible's Grand Narrative* (Downers Grove, IL: IVP Academic, 2006), 378–80. Also see M. Daniel Carroll R., "Old Testament Law, Then and Now: Cultural Boundaries and Moral Identity; Engaging Christopher Wright's Paradigm Approach," *Kairos* 58–59 (2016): 37–59.

5. One debate among scholars who study Old Testament law is whether the shared vocabulary and ideas of these law codes suggest that they stem from a shared Mesopotamian legal tradition.

6. Moshe Weinfeld, *Social Justice in Ancient Israel and in the Ancient Near East* (Minneapolis: Fortress, 1995); J. Gordon McConville, *God and Earthly Power: An Old Testament Political Theology, Genesis–Kings*, Library of Hebrew Bible/Old Testament Studies 454 (London: T&T Clark, 2007); David W. Baker, *Tight Fists or Open Hands? Wealth and Poverty in Old Testament Law* (Grand Rapids: Eerdmans, 2009).

7. Key here is Clifford Geertz. See Geertz, "Local Knowledge: Fact and Law in Comparative Perspective," in *Local Knowledge: Further Essays in Interpretive Anthropology* (New York: Basic Books, 1983), 167–234; Geertz, "Off Echoes: Some Comments on Anthropology and Law," *Political and Legal Anthropology Review* 19, no. 2 (1996): 33–37.

8. Mario Liverani, *International Relations in the Ancient Near East, 1600–1100 BC*, Studies in Diplomacy (New York: Palgrave, 2001), 17–76; Steven Grosby, *Biblical Ideas of Nationality: Ancient and Modern* (Winona Lake, IN: Eisenbrauns, 2002), 120–49.

9. Johanna W. H. van Wijk-Bos, *Making Wise the Simple: The Torah in Christian Faith and Practice* (Grand Rapids: Eerdmans, 2005), 25–32.

10. D. I. Block, "Sojourner," *International Standard Bible Encyclopaedia*, ed. G. W. Bromiley, rev. ed. (Grand Rapids: Eerdmans, 1988), 4:561–64; R. J. D. Knauth, "Alien, Foreign Resident," *Dictionary of the Old Testament: Pentateuch*, ed. T. D. Alexander and D. W. Baker (Downers Grove, IL: InterVarsity, 2003), 26–33; Hans-Georg Wuench, "The Stranger in God's Land—Foreigner, Stranger, Guest: What Can We Learn from Israel's Attitude towards Strangers?," *Old Testament Essays* 27, no. 3 (2014): 1129–54.

11. E.g., Reinhard Achenbach, "*gēr–nåkhrî–tôshav–zār*: Legal and Sacral Distinctions regarding Foreigners in the Pentatech," in *The Foreigner and the Law: Perspectives from the Hebrew Bible and the Ancient Near East*, ed. R. Achenbach, R. Albertz, and J. Wöhle, Beihefte zur Zeitschrift für altorientalische und biblische Rechtsgeschichte 16 (Wiesbaden: Harrassowitz, 2011), 29–51.

12. For surveys of research and proposals, see Mark A. Awabdy, *Immigrants and Innovative Law: Deuteronomy's Theological and Social Vision for the גֵּר*, Forschungen zum Alten Testament 2/67 (Tübingen: Mohr Siebeck, 2014), 15–37; Mark R. Glanville, *Adopting the Stranger as Kindred in Deuteronomy*, Ancient Israel and Its Literature (Atlanta: SBL Press, 2018), 5–41; cf. Markus Zehnder, "Literary and Other Observations on Passages Dealing with Foreigners in the Book of Deuteronomy: The Command to Love the *gēr* in Context," in *Sepher Torath Mosheh: Studies in the Composition and Interpretation of Deuteronomy*, ed. D. I. Block and R. L. Schultz (Peabody, MA: Hendrickson, 2017), 192–231.

13. This is not to deny distinctions, but such an exercise is more appropriate for a technical monograph. For the approach suggested here, see M. Daniel Carroll R., "Welcoming the Stranger: Toward a Theology of Immigration in Deuteronomy," in *For Our Good Always: Studies on the Message and Influence of Deuteronomy in Honor of Daniel I. Block*, ed. J. S. DeRouchie, J. Gile, and K. J. Turner (Winona Lake, IN: Eisenbrauns, 2013), 441–61; Jacob Milgrom, *Leviticus 17–22*, Anchor Bible 3A (New York: Doubleday, 2000), 1416–20; Jeremiah Unterman, *Justice for All: How the Jewish Bible Revolutionized Ethics* (Philadelphia: Jewish Publication Society, 2017), 41–62; cf. Mark W. Hamilton, *Jesus, King of Strangers: What the Bible Really Says about Immigration* (Grand Rapids: Eerdmans, 2019), 81–97.

14. There are exceptions to this generalization. *Zār* can refer to lay Israelites who are not Levites (Exod. 29:33; Lev. 22:10–13; Num. 1:51; 3:10, 38); they are "foreign" in the sense that they are not qualified to do what only the priests can perform.

15. Selected verses: *nokrî* (feminine, *nokriyyâ*): the licentious woman (Prov. 6:24; 23:27), foreign women (1 Kings 11:1; Ezra 10:2; Neh. 13:26); *nēkār*: other gods (Josh. 24:20; 1 Sam. 7:3; Jer. 5:19; Mal. 2:11); *ben-nēkār*: followers of other gods (Ezek. 44:7–9), enemies (Ps. 18:44–45 [18:45–46 MT]). *Zār*: enemies

(Ps. 54:3 [54:5 MT]; Isa. 1:7; 29:5; Jer. 5:19; 51:51; Hos. 7:9), foreign gods (Deut. 32:16; Jer. 2:25), an adulterous woman (Prov. 22:14). *Nokrî/nokriyyâ* and *zār* appear in parallel, referring to, for example, an immoral woman (Prov. 2:16; 5:20; 7:5) or enemies (Obad. 11). *Nēkār* and *zār* occur together in Jer. 5:19.

16. In passages such as Prov. 6:1 and 11:15, readers wonder whether the "stranger" is an individual who is not well known or a literal foreigner. If the latter, then these passages are a warning not to do business with these foreigners.

17. Lev. 25:23, 1 Chron. 29:15, and Ps. 39:12 (39:13 MT) also have this pairing, but as a metaphorical reference to the experience of Israelites.

18. Some scholars argue that the term refers to Israelites who fled south to Judah after the Assyrian conquest of 722–720 BC or to internally displaced people from within Judah in the aftermath of Sennacherib's invasion of 701 or to internal casualties of the economic realities brought on by the monarchy (e.g., taxation, urbanization, rise of a privileged class). For surveys, see Awabdy, *Immigrants and Innovative Law*, 15–24, 108–16; Glanville, *Adopting the Stranger as Kindred in Deuteronomy*, 7–14, 33–41, passim.

19. The English versions are not always consistent in their translations, but their primary options are these: "alien" or "resident alien" or "stranger" (New Revised Standard Version); "foreigner" (New International Version, Holman Christian Standard Bible); "sojourner" or "stranger" (English Standard Version); "immigrant" (Common English Bible).

20. The best example of this difference is found in the passages that condemn intermarriage in Ezra 9–10 and Neh. 13. They use *nokrî* and *zār*, never *gēr*, to refer to the women rejected by Israel's leaders.

21. Christiana van Houten, *The Alien in Israelite Law*, Journal for the Study of the Old Testament Supplement Series 107 (Sheffield: Sheffield Academic Press, 1991), 34–42; José E. Ramírez Kidd, *Alterity and Identity in Israel*, Beihefte zur Zeitschrift für die alttestamentliche Wissenschaft 283 (Berlin: de Gruyter, 1999), 110–16; Snell, *Flight and Freedom in the Ancient Near East*, 87–98. For the Laws of Eshnunna and Code of Hammurabi, see Hallo, *Context of Scripture*, 2:332–35 and 335–53, respectively. While racism was generally absent in Mesopotamia, there was prejudice against the Gutians and Amorites. See Jerrold S. Cooper, *The Curse of Agade* (Baltimore: Johns Hopkins University Press, 1983), 30–33; Brian Rainey, *Religion, Ethnicity and Xenophobia in the Bible: A Theoretical, Exegetical and Theological Study*, Routledge Studies in the Biblical World (New York: Routledge, 2019), 54–95.

22. Nicholas Wolterstorff, *Justice: Rights and Wrongs* (Princeton: Princeton University Press, 2008), 75–82. This grouping apparently also appears in a recently discovered piece of pottery at Khirbet Qeiyafa from the 10th century BC. See Bob Becking and Paul Sanders, "Plead for the Poor and the Widow: The Ostracon from Khirbet Qeiyafa as Expression of Social Consciousnessness," *Zeitschrift für altorientalische und biblische Rechtsgeschichte* 17 (2011): 133–48; Reinhard Achenbach, "The Protection of *Personae Miserae*

in Ancient Israelite Law and Wisdom in the Ostracon from Khirbet Qeiyafa," *Semitica* 54 (2012): 93–125. Levites are sometimes included in these measures because the law restricts them from owning property (Deut. 14:27–29; 16:11, 14; 26:12–13). The verb *gûr* (I) is applied to them (they "sojourn" in the land; Deut. 18:6), but the noun *gēr* is never applied to Levites.

23. See especially A. J. Culp, *Memoir of Moses: The Literary Creation of Covenantal Memory in Deuteronomy* (Lanham, MA: Lexington/Fortress Academic, 2019).

24. In the Septuagint, the primary term used for the Hebrew word *gēr* is *prosēlytos*, from which we get "proselyte." Apparently this word was created to refer to non-Israelites who had integrated themselves into Israelite society, including the embrace of its religion. In time, it came to mean those outsiders who had been circumcised. See *"prosēlytos"* in *New International Dictionary of New Testament Theology and Exegesis*, ed. M. Silva (Grand Rapids: Zondervan, 2014), 4:47–50.

25. See Exod. 12:19, 49; Lev. 16:29; 17:15; 18:26; 19:34; 24:16, 22; Num. 9:14; 15:29–30; cf. Lev. 25:35.

26. For the distinctions in rituals in Leviticus, see Mark A. Awabdy, "Green Eggs and Shawarma: Reinterpreting the Bible, Reforming Mission, and Leviticus' *gēr* as a Test Case," *Asbury Journal* 66, no. 1 (2011): 31–45. For a discussion of Deut. 23:3–8 (23:4–9 MT), see Carroll R., "Welcoming the Stranger," 453–54.

27. David G. Firth, *Including the Stranger: Foreigners in the Former Prophets*, New Studies in Biblical Theology 50 (Downers Grove, IL: IVP Academic, 2019); cf. Adrianne Leveen, *Biblical Narratives of Israelites and Their Neighbors: Strangers at the Gate*, Routledge Interdisciplinary Perspectives on Biblical Criticism (New York: Routledge, 2017).

28. The Targum on Ruth 1:4–5 says that Naomi's two sons died prematurely because they married Moabite women.

29. For the redemption of property and whether levirate marriage is in view, see Robert L. Hubbard Jr., *Ruth*, New International Commentary on the Old Testament (Grand Rapids: Eerdmans, 1988), 48–63; Tamara Cohn Eskanazi and Tikva Frymer-Kensky, *Ruth*, JPS Bible Commentary (Philadelphia: Jewish Publication Society, 2011), xxviii–xxxviii, liii–lv. For the theology, see Hubbard, *Ruth*, 63–74; Eskanazi and Frymer-Kensky, *Ruth*, xlviii–lv; Daniel Hawk, *Ruth*, Apollos Old Testament Commentary 7B (Downers Grove, IL: InterVarsity Press, 2015), 39–43; Eunny Lee, "Women's Doings in Ruth: A Feminist Biblical Theology of Providence," in *After Exegesis: Feminist Biblical Theology* (Waco: Baylor University Press, 2015), 31–43.

30. Dianne Bergant, "Ruth: The Migrant Who Saved the People," in *Migration, Religious Experience, and Globalization*, ed. G. Campese and P. Ciallella (New York: Center for Migration Studies, 2003), 49–61; Gale A. Yee, "'She Stood in Tears amid the Alien Corn': Ruth, the Perpetual Foreigner and Model Minority," in *They Were All Together in One Place? Toward Minority Biblical*

Criticism, ed. R. C. Bailey, T. B. Liew, and F. F. Segovia, Semeia 57 (Atlanta: Society of Biblical Literature, 2009), 119–40; Agnethe Siquans, "Foreignness and Poverty in the Book of Ruth: A Legal Way for a Poor Foreign Woman to Be Integrated into Israel," *Journal of Biblical Literature* 128, no. 3 (2009): 443–52; John Mansford Prior, "'Failed' Migrants Return: A Transforming Word from the Book of Ruth," in *God's People on the Move: Biblical and Global Perspectives on Migration and Mission*, ed. V. Nguyen and J. M. Prior (Eugene, OR: Pickwick, 2014), 132–43. See the article "Refugees," by Celestin Musekura, inserted into the commentary on Ruth in *Africa Bible Commentary*, ed. T. Adeyemo (Nairobi: WordAlive Publishers, 2006), 321.

31. See Richard Alba and Victor Nee, "Assimilation," in *The New Americans: A Guide to Immigration Since 1965*, ed. M. C. Waters and R. Ueda (Cambridge, MA: Harvard University Press, 2007), 124–36. For Ruth, see M. Daniel Carroll R., "Once a Stranger, Always a Stranger? Immigration, Assimilation, and the Book of Ruth," *International Bulletin of Missionary Research* 39, no. 4 (2015): 185–88; cf. Katherine E. Southwood, "Will Naomi's Nation Be Ruth's Nation? Ethnic Translation as a Metaphor for Ruth's Assimilation within Judah," *Humanities* 3 (2014): 102–31. Others using social sciences include Bonnie Honig, "Ruth, the Model Émigrée: Mourning and the Symbolic Politics of Immigration," *Political Theory* 25, no. 1 (1997): 112–36; Neil Glover, "Your People, My People: An Exploration of Ethnicity in Ruth," *Journal for the Study of the Old Testament* 33, no. 3 (2009): 293–313; Victor H. Matthews, "The Determination of Social Identity in the Story of Ruth," in *The Family in Life and in Death: The Family in Ancient Israel; Sociological and Archaeological Perspectives*, ed. P. Dutcher-Walls, Library of Biblical Studies/Old Testament Studies 504 (New York: T&T Clark, 2009), 16–27.

32. *Nokrî* also occurs in Isa. 60:10 and 61:5 (along with *zār*), which speak of judgment on the nations who had cruelly oppressed the people of God. In these verses, the negative connotation of "foreign" reappears.

33. This is the contention of Hoffmeier, *The Immigration Crisis*, who links legal foreign resident immigrants with the *gēr* and links the undocumented foreigner with *nokrî* and *zār*.

34. Mark R. Amstutz, *Just Immigration: American Policy in Christian Perspective* (Grand Rapids: Eerdmans, 2017). Other aspects are at play in these observations, such as the divide between communitarian and cosmopolitan approaches. For a different perspective, see Tisha M. Rajendra, *Migrants and Citizens: Justice and Responsibility in the Ethics of Immigration* (Grand Rapids: Eerdmans, 2017).

Chapter 3 Entertaining Angels Unawares: Hospitality for the Stranger in the New Testament

1. The number of resources is immense. See, for example, Darrell L. Bock and Gregory J. Herrick, *Jesus in Context: Background Readings for*

Gospel Study (Grand Rapids: Baker Academic, 2005); Richard Bauckham, *Jesus and the Eyewitnesses: The Gospels as Eyewitness Testimony* (Grand Rapids: Eerdmans, 2006); Darrell L. Bock and J. Ed Komoszewski, eds., *Jesus, Skepticism, and the Problem of History: Criteria and Context in the Study of Christian Origins* (Grand Rapids: Zondervan, 2019); Craig S. Keener, *Christobiography: Memory, History, and the Reliability of the Gospels* (Grand Rapids: Eerdmans, 2019).

2. Other passages could be examined, such as the parable of the day laborers in Matt. 20:1–16 (see Jean-Pierre Ruiz, *Readings from the Edges: The Bible and People on the Move* [Maryknoll, NY: Orbis, 2011], 115–22).

3. Richard T. France, "Herod and the Children of Bethlehem," *Novum Testamentum* 21, no. 2 (1979): 98–120; Craig S. Keener, *A Commentary on the Gospel of Matthew* (Grand Rapids: Eerdmans, 1999), 110–11 (see his excursus on the magi on p. 99); Bock and Herrick, *Jesus in Context*, 52–54. It is reported that Augustus said in a pun (in Greek) that it was better to be Herod's pig (*hys*) than his son (*hyios*).

4. Clinton E. Arnold, "Matthew," in *Zondervan Illustrated Bible Backgrounds Commentary: New Testament* (Grand Rapids: Zondervan, 2002), 1:17.

5. Craig L. Blomberg, *Jesus and the Gospels: An Introduction and Survey*, 2nd ed. (Nashville: B&H Academic, 2009), 8–81; Eckhard J. Schnabel, *Early Christian Mission*, vol. 1, *Jesus and the Twelve* (Downers Grove, IL: InterVarsity), 177–206.

6. H. G. M. Williamson, "Samaritans," *Dictionary of Jesus and the Gospels*, ed. Joel B. Green, Scot McKnight, and I. Howard Marshall (Downers Grove, IL: InterVarsity, 1992), 724–28; Robert T. Anderson and Terry Giles, *The Keepers: An Introduction to the History and Culture of the Samaritans* (Grand Rapids: Baker Academic, 2001).

7. Schnabel, *Early Christian Mission*, 1:242–47, 260–62.

8. Bock and Herrick, *Jesus in Context*, 212.

9. Darrell L. Bock, *Luke,* Baker Exegetical Commentary on the New Testament (Grand Rapids: Baker Academic, 1996), 2:1405–6.

10. Craig L. Blomberg, *Interpreting the Parables*, 2nd ed. (Downers Grove, IL: InterVarsity, 2012), 295–302; cf. Bock, *Luke*, 2:1018–35.

11. Regarding the Old Testament, note these examples of use in Matt. 25: the sheep and goats (cf. Ezek. 34:17), the "Son of Man" (cf. Dan. 7:13), and coming with the angels (cf. Zech. 14:5). For Jewish texts, see Bock and Herrick, *Jesus in Context*, 183–85.

12. See "*xenos*," *New International Dictionary*, 3:442–46. The term occurs 14 times in the New Testament.

13. For a helpful list of these passages, see Klyne Snodgrass, *Stories with Intent: A Comprehensive Guide to the Parables of Jesus* (Grand Rapids: Eerdmans, 2008), 544–49.

14. W. D. Davies and Dale C. Allison, *A Critical and Exegetical Commentary on the Gospel of Saint Matthew*, International Critical Commentary

(Edinburgh: T&T Clark, 1997), 3:422–23; Snodgrass, *Stories with Intent*, 551–63; cf. Ernesto Cardenal, "The Last Judgment (Matt. 25:31–46)," in *The Gospel in Solentiname*, trans. Donald D. Walsh (Maryknoll, NY: Orbis, 1982), 4:49–60.

15. For "little ones" and "the least" (the superlative of "little ones"), see Matt. 5:19; 10:42; 11:11; 18:6, 10, 14. For "brothers and/or sisters" (or the like) as disciples, see 5:22–24, 47; 7:3–5; 12:48–50; 18:15, 21, 35; 23:8; 28:10; as Jesus's siblings, see 12:46–47; 13:55; as the siblings of others, see 1:2, 11; 4:18, 21; 10:2, 21; 14:3; 17:1; 19:29; 20:24–25.

16. Ulrich Luz, *Matthew 21–28*, trans. J. E. Crouch, Hermeneia (Minneapolis: Fortress, 2005), 267–84; R. T. France, *The Gospel of Matthew*, New International Commentary on the New Testament (Grand Rapids: Eerdmans, 2007), 953–63; Darrell L. Bock and Benjamin I. Simpson, *Jesus according to Scripture: Restoring the Portrait from the Gospels*, 2nd ed. (Grand Rapids: Baker Academic, 2017), 454–56; Craig L. Blomberg, *A New Testament Theology* (Waco: Baylor University Press, 2018), 377–80.

17. Craig L. Blomberg, *Matthew*, New American Commentary 22 (Nashville: Broadman & Holman, 1992), 377–80; Craig S. Keener, *A Commentary on the Gospel of Matthew* (Grand Rapids: Eerdmans, 1999), 604–6.

18. Note Aquiles Ernesto Martínez in "Jesus, the Immigrant Child: A Diasporic Reading of Matthew 2:1–23," *Apuntes* 26, no. 3 (2006): 84–114; Ched Myers and Matthew Colwell, *Our God Is Undocumented: Biblical Faith and Immigrant Justice* (St. Louis: Chalice, 2012), 159–77. Deirdre Cornell, in *Jesus Was a Migrant* (Maryknoll, NY: Orbis, 2014), 95–102, connects Jesus the migrant with *las posadas* at Christmastime within Hispanic Catholic tradition.

19. See *"dēmos"* (for *"parepidēmos"*) and *"paroikos,"* in *New International Dictionary*, 1:685 and 3:642–45, respectively; cf. John H. Elliott, *1 Peter*, Anchor Bible 37B (New York: Doubleday, 2000), 476–83.

20. For the complexities related to Roman identity and citizenship, see Benjamin H. Dunning, *Aliens and Sojourners: Self as Other in Early Christianity*, Divinations: Reading Later Ancient Religion (Philadelphia: University of Pennsylvania Press, 2009), 25–45.

21. Those who argue for some kind of sociopolitical explanation, although with distinct reconstructions, include John H. Elliott, *A Home for the Homeless: A Sociological Exegesis of 1 Peter, Its Situation and Strategy* (Minneapolis: Fortress, 1990), 37–100; Elliott, *1 Peter*; Karen H. Jobes, *1 Peter*, Baker Exegetical Commentary on the New Testament (Grand Rapids: Baker Academic, 2005), 28–42, 61–66; Shively T. J. Smith, *Strangers to Family: Diaspora and 1 Peter's Invention of God's Household* (Waco: Baylor University Press, 2016), 17–43. For a spiritual explanation, see Thomas R. Schreiner, *1, 2 Peter, Jude*, New American Commentary 37 (Nashville: Broadman & Holman, 2003), 37–41. Note the thoughtful reflections in Miroslav Volf, "Soft Difference: Theological Reflections on the Relation between Church and Culture in 1 Peter," *Ex Auditu* 10 (1994): 15–30.

22. Dunning, *Aliens and Sojourners*, 46–63. For a recent use of 1 Peter and the book of Hebrews as applying to modern realities, see Jennifer T. Kaalund, *Reading Hebrews and 1 Peter with the African American Great Migration*, Library of New Testament Studies 598 (London: T&T Clark, 2019).

23. The reader will notice inconsistency in the NIV translation of the relevant terms, with the same Greek term being rendered with different English words. This is true as well of other English versions.

24. For the identity of the recipients of the Epistle of James, see Douglas J. Moo, *The Letter of James*, Pillar New Testament Commentary (Grand Rapids: Eerdmans, 2000); Dan G. McCartney, *James*, Baker Exegetical Commentary on the New Testament (Grand Rapids: Baker Academic, 2009), 32–37; Scot McKnight, *The Letter of James*, New International Commentary on the New Testament (Grand Rapids: Eerdmans, 2011), 65–68.

25. These sections of the Epistle are from Dunning, *Aliens and Sojourners*, 65–66. He provides a fuller discussion on this discourse on pp. 64–67.

26. This title for God and this discussion are drawn from Peter C. Phan, "*Deus Migrator*: God the Migrant; Migration of Theology and Theology of Migration," *Theological Studies* 77, no. 4 (2016): 845–68.

27. Austin P. Flannery, ed., *Documents of Vatican II* (Grand Rapids: Eerdmans, 1975), 407–13.

28. Enoch Wan, *Diaspora Missiology: Theory, Methodology, and Practice* (Portland, OR: Institute of Diaspora Studies, 2011); Sadiri Joy, ed., *The Human Tidal Wave: Global Migration, Megacities, Multiculturalism, Pluralism, Diaspora Missiology* (Manila: LifeChange Publishing, 2013); Sadiri Joy and Tesunao Yamamori, eds., *Scattered and Gathered: A Global Compendium of Diaspora Missiology* (Oxford: Regnum, 2016).

29. Note, e.g., Jehu Hanciles, *Beyond Christendom: Globalization, African Migration, and the Transformation of the West* (Maryknoll, NY: Orbis, 2008); Elaine Padilla and Peter C. Phan, eds., *Christianities in Migration: The Global Perspective*, Christianities of the World (New York: Palgrave Macmillan, 2016).

30. Christine D. Pohl, "Responding to Strangers: Insights from the Christian Tradition," *Studies in Christian Ethics* 19, no. 1 (2006): 81–101; Joshua W. Jipp, *Saved by Faith and Hospitality* (Grand Rapids: Eerdmans, 2017); J. T. Fitzgerald, "Hospitality," in *Dictionary of New Testament Background*, ed. C. A. Evans and S. E. Porter (Downers Grove, IL: InterVarsity, 2000), 522–25.

31. Daniel G. Groody, "Fruit of the Vine and Work of Human Hands: Immigration and the Eucharist," in *A Promised Land, A Perilous Journey: Theological Perspectives on Migration*, ed. D. G. Groody and G. Campese (Notre Dame, IN: University of Notre Dame Press, 2008), 299–315; Craig Wong, "The Subversive Act of Breaking Bread: How the Eucharist Transforms the Immigration Discussion," in *Religion and Politics in America's Borderlands*, ed. Sarah Azaransky (Lanham, MD: Lexington, 2013), 145–61;

Michael Rhodes, "'Forward unto Virtue': Formative Practices and 1 Corinthians 11:17–34," *Journal of Theological Interpretation* 11, no. 1 (2017): 119–38.

32. An extensive theological treatment of this tension on immigration issues appears in *Immigrants among Us: A Lutheran Framework for Addressing Immigration Issues*, A Report of the Commission on Theology and Church Relations, The Lutheran Church—Missouri Synod (St. Louis: Concordia, 2012). This report is also available in Spanish. For a different Lutheran reflection, see Peter C. Meilaender, *Toward a Theory of Immigration* (New York: Palgrave, 2001).

Epilogue: The Scriptures and the Future

1. Richard S. Briggs, *The Virtuous Reader: Old Testament Narrative and Interpretive Virtue*, Studies in Theological Interpretation (Grand Rapids: Baker Academic, 2010).

Scripture Index

139

Subject Index